MUSIC AND FOOD OF
SPAIN

By

S H A R O N O ' C O N N O R

Spanish Menu Cookbook

Classical Spanish Guitar Music

Menus and Music Productions, Inc.
Piedmont, California

Copyright© 1993 by Menus and Music Productions, Inc.
Map copyright© 1993 by John Coreris

Library of Congress Cataloging-in-Publication Data
O'Connor, Sharon
Menus and Music Volume VI
Music and Food of Spain
Spanish Menu Cookbook
Classical Spanish Guitar Music

Includes Index
1. Cookery 2. Entertaining
I. Title
93-078502
ISBN 0-9615150-9-0, 0-9615150-4-X

Menus and Music is published by
Menus and Music Productions, Inc.
1462 66th Street
Emeryville, CA 94608
(510) 482-4800

Book and cover design by HS Design
Cover photograph courtesy of Hostal de La Gavina

Manufactured in the United States of America
10 9 8 7 6 5 4 3

MUSIC AND FOOD OF
SPAIN

Contents

Introduction

I fell in love with Spain twenty years ago. I was studying music at the Amsterdam Conservatory of Music when I escaped from my studies and the gray skies of a Dutch winter to the sunshine and warmth of the Spanish island of Ibiza. I felt instantly at home there and elsewhere in Spain, probably because so much of the countryside reminded me of my home in California. I learned to cook quite a few dishes while living on Ibiza and later enjoyed many cafes and restaurants in the city of Barcelona. The beauty of Spain and its wonderful food were a highlight of my first trip to Europe.

While collecting recipes for this book, our family traveled throughout Spain. We were constantly amazed at the amount of enjoyment the Spanish pack into every day. Everyone seems to be eating and enjoying themselves at cafes and restaurants at all hours of the day and on into the night. We once pulled into a small town at midnight and were worried there would be no one awake to ask directions to our hotel. We shouldn't have worried: Most of the town was still outside, in the middle of their evening meal!

When we returned to California, the streets of our home town seemed strangely quiet—where were all the people sitting at outdoor cafes animatedly discussing the events of the day?

Recipes for this book have been sent to me from Spain and fine Spanish restaurants in the United States over a two-year period. Translations from

Spanish, Catalán, and Basque have been a time-consuming yet rewarding part of this project. I received generous help in deciphering cooking terms from local Spanish chefs and at the same time enjoyed great times with them. The recipes from Spanish restaurants in the United States are mostly traditional, but many have been adapted by the chefs to use local ingredients and to reflect the different ethnic cuisines the chefs have encountered in the United States. During the past two years, the chefs that contributed to this book have earned my deepest respect, and I hope you too will appreciate their talent, expertise, and creativity.

In your home kitchen you may need or want to adapt these recipes by substituting ingredients. Any experienced cook uses taste, smell, and feel rather than precise measurements and the rigid acceptance of exact ingredients. Some of the best dishes I've ever made happened when I adapted a recipe to emphasize the tastiest ingredient I brought home from the market that day, or when I didn't have an ingredient and substituted another. Add two onions instead of one, use a little less sugar, add extra tomatoes—this is the kind of creativity that makes cooking fun!

The Spanish contributors to this book will provide you with a connoisseur's guide to exceptional inns and restaurants of Spain. All of them are members of Relais & Chateaux, a thirty-nine-year-old association of 411 individual hotels and restaurants worldwide. These privately owned accommodations reflect the personality and dedication of the hotelier as well as the heritage of the region in which they are located. Relais & Chateaux members maintain very high standards in order to retain their memberships, as they are reviewed annually. They share a steadfast commitment to the five C's of Relais & Chateaux hospitality: character, courtesy, calm, charm, and cuisine.

As is true of most cellists I know, one of my heroes is the great Catalán cellist and humanitarian, Pablo Casals, so performing the three Catalán folksongs for this project was a dream come true. The Spanish pieces recorded here by guitarist Marc Teicholz are gems of the guitar repertoire. They may be enjoyed as relaxing dinner music or as a beautiful after dinner concert. Although Spanish food is quite regional, the country is united in its love of the guitar. I hope this music will make you, too, love Spain.

A meal should engage all of the senses. Taste, of course, is primary, but aroma, color, texture, and of course, sound should be a part of the enjoyment. I hope this volume of Menus and Music will help you create and enjoy a great Spanish dinner! *Que aproveche!*

—Sharon O'Connor

Music Notes

There exists a legend regarding the origin of the guitar that is more beautifully suggestive than historic fact: Apollo was running in pursuit of a beautiful nymph, gallantly repeating to her all the while: "Don't tire yourself, I promise not to catch up with you." When, finally, he did succeed in taking her into his arms, she called out to her semidivine father, who instantly changed her into a laurel tree. Apollo made the first guitar from the wood of this tree and gave it as form the graceful, curved contours that forever reveal its feminine origin. That is why the guitar is of a reserved and changeable nature, even hysterical at time; but that is also why it is sweet and smooth, harmonious and delicate. When it is played with love and skill, there issues from its melancholy sounds a rapture that holds us fast to it forever.

—Andrés Segovia

The guitar is deeply Spanish. It was slow to establish itself in northern Europe, where it was seen as an instrument for the lower classes. In 1619 the German composer and theoretician Michael Praetorius described it dismissively as an instrument "for strumming, to which villanelles and other foolish, trashy songs are sung." In Spain, however, during the same period a Spaniard who played the guitar was regarded as the epitome of a nobleman. After 1800, with the contributions of the great guitarists Sor, Giulani, and Tárrega, the guitar began to establish itself as a solo instrument in Vienna, Paris, and London, the musical centers of Europe. During the period of Romantic music in the late 1800s and early 19th century, however, the guitar was displaced by the piano. A renaissance of guitar music took place in the 1930s when performances by Andrés Segovia and compositions by the Spanish composers recorded here transformed the old romantic guitar into a solo instrument for the concert stage. Today there is an extensive concert repertoire for the Spanish guitar that is beloved throughout the world.

Isaac Albéniz (1860-1909)

"Asturias" from *Suite Española*
Capricho Catalán, Op. 165

Albéniz was a musical child prodigy who had an extraordinary career as a piano virtuoso. He was also a composer of numerous expressive and virtuosic works for piano. During his career Albéniz turned more and more to Spanish folk music as the basis for his compositions. The great guitarist Francisco Tarrega made guitar transcriptions of Albéniz's piano works. There is an appealing but undocumented tale that upon hearing Tarrega's rendering of some of his piano compositions, Albéniz declared that the music had found its rightful home on guitar.

Included among Albéniz's virtuoso piano pieces is "Asturias" from his *Suite Española*. "Asturias" is now performed more often on the guitar than the piano and is a standard of the guitar repertoire.

Henri Collet, in his book *Albeniz et Granados* (Paris, 1948), relates that the Catalonian Albéniz remarked to friends, "I am a Moor" and added "I do not feel Catalonian but find myself at home in Andalucía." In the Capricho Catalán recorded here, Albeniz combines a Catalonian melody with a bass in the rhythm of the Andalusian *zambra*.

Manuel de Falla (1876-1946)

La Vida Breve
"Asturianna,""Nana," and "Canción"
from *Siete Canciones Populares Españolas*

Falla, along with his elder contemporaries Albéniz and Granados, was one of the first Spanish composers in three centuries to win international renown. He was influenced by his French colleagues Debussy and Ravel, but his art remained embedded in the folk music of Spain. His most famous pieces are *El Amor Brujo*, a ballet with songs; *Noches en los Jardines de España*, a suite of three symphonic impressions for piano and orchestra; and *El Sombrero*, a ballet with designs by Pablo Picasso. *La Vida Breve*, Falla's only opera, was written in 1905. The three Spanish songs recorded here are "Nana," an Andalusian lullaby of exceptional tenderness and beauty; "Canción," a bright and charming song portraying the more light-hearted side of Spanish art and life; and "Asturianna," a dark-hued piece that evokes the romantic spirit of Spain. This last song is based on a dreamlike story: A maiden seeks consolation under a pine tree; she weeps, and the tree also weeps in compassion.

Francisco Tárrega (1852-1909)

"Recuerdos de la Alhambra"

Tarrega became a guitarist when the guitar was overshadowed by the louder and more resonant piano. He acquired an unusually resonant guitar designed and constructed by Antonio Torres. With this superior instrument, Tarrega paved the way for the rebirth of the guitar in the twentieth century. He performed his own compositions, and transcribed the works of his friends Albéniz and Granados as well as movements from Beethoven piano sonatas and preludes by Chopin. His own romantic compositions are now in almost every guitarist's concert repertoire. Tarrega's most famous solo for guitar is the one recorded here, "Recuerdos de la Alhambra," or "Memories of the Alhambra." The guitar tremolo (a tremulous effect produced by the rapid reiteration of the same tone) of this piece alludes to the water flowing from the fountains of this famous garden in Granada.

Joaquin Turina (1882-1949)
Sevillana, Op. 29
Fandanguillo, Op. 36

Turina was born in Seville and for most of his adult life taught guitar and composition at the Royal Conservatory in Madrid. Sevillana, composed in 1923, consists of brilliant arpeggios, *rasguedado* (strumming), and *cante hondo* (flamenco song) and is a tribute to the spirited flamenco dances of Seville. Fandanguillo, composed in 1925, is dedicated to the great guitarist Andrés Segovia. Varied tone colors and percussive elements merge to make up an impressionistic meditation on another dance of Spain, the fandango. It has become a favorite of the guitar repertoire.

Federico Mompou (1893-1987)
Preludio from *Suite Compostelana*

Mompou was born in Barcelona and is one of the great Catalán musicians of the twentieth century. He studied compositon in Paris, where he lived for twenty years before returning to Catalunya. *Suite Compostelana*, composed in 1962, pays homage to the ancient city of Santiago de Compostela, where Segovia and other international musicians gathered each summer to teach and perform, perpetuating the rich traditions of Spanish music. Preludio is a clear and simple piece that is typical of Mompou's compositional style of maximum expressiveness with minimum means.

Enrique Granados (1867-1916)
La Maja de Goya

La Maja de Goya is one of the "*tonadillas, escritas en stile antiguo*" ("little songs written in the old style") that are part of a song cycle Granados wrote in an eighteenth-century style. Granados, who had a lifelong admiration for the great painter Goya, once declared, "I am not a musician, but an artist." This piece conveys a tender and restrained atmosphere.

Anonymous
"El Noy de la Mare"
Traditional Catalán folksong (arranged by Miguel Llobet)

A traditional and popular Catalán folk song about the infant Jesus.

Ernesto Halffter (1905-1990)
"*Danza de la Pastora*"

Ernesto Halffter was a composer and conductor from a Spanish family of musicians of German origin. "Danza de la Pastora" is taken from his notably successful ballet, *Sonatina*, composed in 1928. He was a pupil and close friend of Manuel de Falla, and after Falla's death he completed and later revised his teacher's composition, *L'Atlantida*. Halffter conducted orchestras throughout Spain, in Paris, and South America, and he also was the director of the Seville Conservatory.

Joaquín Malats (1872-1912)
Serenata Española

Born in Barcelona, Malats became a well-known composer and pianist. A winner of the Paris Conservatory prize, he was one of the first and best interpreters of Albeniz's most famous work, *Iberia*. He composed piano pieces as well as the orchestral piece *Impressions de España*, of which the elegant serenade recorded here is a part.

Cook's Notes

Traditional eating habits have not changed much in Spain over the centuries and are quite unlike those of the rest of Europe. After a small breakfast, possibly a *cafe con leche* with toast or *churros*, most people eat a second breakfast in the late morning: coffee and a sweet roll, a sandwich, or an omelette. The tapas bars open at one o'clock, serving snacks of crisply fried anchovies, prawns, or a few slices of ham with bread and sherry to stave off hunger until lunch, which is eaten at two o'clock. The midday meal is often the largest of the day and is followed by a siesta in hot weather before the return to work in the late afternoon. Lunch consists of at least three courses: a starter such as a soup, egg dish, vegetable dish, or salad; a main course of meat or fish that is often accompanied by potatoes; and a dessert consisting usually of fresh fruit or pudding. Late afternoon is the time for a snack of pastry, cake, or a tart with coffee or tea. In the evening the tapas bars fill again when the shops close about eight. Supper is after that, and it might begin as late as 11 P.M.

Of course food is more than nourishment in Spain. It is connected to the country's art, literature, craft, and history: the culmination of centuries of tradition. There has certainly been a good deal of cross-fertilization in Spanish culinary history. The Romans brought Spanish olive oil, figs, grapes, wine, and fish to Rome, and the Roman colonizers contributed to Spain the *cocido*, a boiled dinner of meats, sausages, and vegetables that is still enjoyed throughout the country today. The Moors ruled the Iberian peninsula for more than seven centuries during a golden age of science, literature, philosophy, and art, and they also exerted a strong influence on the food of Spain. They brought irrigation systems that turned barren regions into agricultural land, and introduced the cultivation of rice, sugar cane, and many fruits and vegetables. The Moors and the Sephardim Jews brought the exotic spice saffron, honeyed sweets and pastries, and savory dishes with fruits and almonds. It is this Moorish influence that distinguishes Spanish food from that of the rest of Europe. The discovery of the Americas brought tomatoes, potatoes, peppers, beans, squash, avocados, corn, and chocolate, which were then introduced to Europe from Spain.

Spanish food emphasizes subtle flavorings and interesting combinations of fresh ingredients. The wealth and variety of produce, fish, and meats in Spain would delight any chef. Spanish culinary customs are determined basically by the regional geography of Spain, and these are best characterized by the Spanish saying: "In the north you stew; in the central region, you roast; in the east you simmer, and in the south you fry."

MAP OF SPAIN

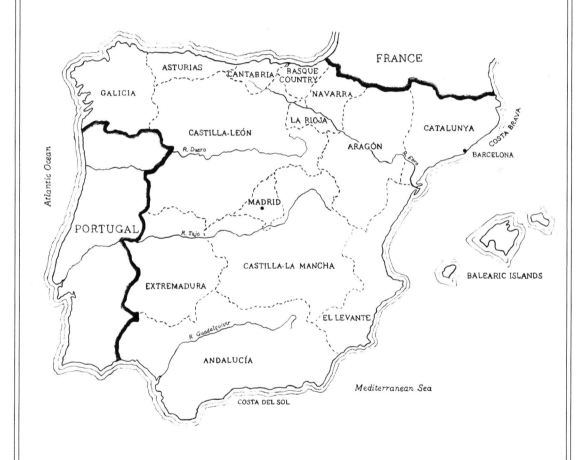

Asturias

The countryside of Asturias, with its green meadows and forests of oaks and chestnuts, seems like a part of Brittany, Normandy, or Ireland. In fact, it was settled by Celts. This is the one area of Spain that was never conquered by the Moors, and it was from Asturias that the Christian reconquest of Spain began. The most famous dish of Asturias is the *fabada asturianna*, a bean stew. This makes perfect sense, because during the bitter cold winters of the region, all life centers around the hearth where the beans bubble over the fire. The rivers of Asturias provide excellent trout and salmon, and the Bay of Biscay a wonderful selection of seafood. Apples are also plentiful, and hard cider is the quintessential Asturian drink.

Cantabria

This region's fertile meadows, mountainous interior, and extensive rocky coastline are similar to those of Asturias and the Basque lands. The fishing, cattle, and agriculture of Cantabria are reflected in the region's cuisine, which is noted for seafood, meat, and excellent cheeses.

Galicia

Galicia, settled by the Celts, is situated at the topmost western corner of Spain and hardly seems related to the rest of the country. It was once called Finisterre, the end of the world, beyond which roared the winds of the unknown. Galicia was also Spain's first tourist center. During the Middle Ages Santiago de Compostela was a pilgrimage almost as important as Rome and Jerusalem. The sea scallop, still the basis of a frequently enjoyed meal in Galicia, is called the pilgrim's shell because it was collected by pilgrims who considered it a symbol of Saint James. The fat livestock grazing on the region's lush green pastures provide excellent meat and dairy products. Butter and lard are used in cooking more often than olive oil, unlike the rest of Spain. Another specialty is the empanada, a turnover filled with meat and vegetables.

The Basque Country

The Basque Country consists of three provinces: Vizcaya, Guipúzcoa, and Alava. Beginning at the end of the Bay of Biscay and straddling the Pyrenees, the region has a long tradition of self-sufficiency and democratic ways. The origin of the Basque language is unknown and, although it borrows from both French and Spanish, the language has no relation to either one. There is a tale that acknowledges the impossibility of the language and the assertiveness of the women: The devil decided he wanted to learn Basque. He hid himself behind the door in a Basque kitchen to listen. At the end of a whole year, he had learned only two words in Basque, "Yes, ma'am."

The Basque take their cooking and eating very seriously, and it is here that Spain's answer to nouvelle cuisine was born. *La nueva cocina vasca* has adapted traditional recipes to modern tastes and imaginatively uses old products in new ways and new products in old ways.

La Rioja

The great Ebro River flows through La Rioja, and its vast fertile valley and the region's good climate provide ideal agricultural conditions. Of course, Rioja is primarily known as the wine-producing region of Spain, and this region is the country's largest producer of quality red wines. Like most good wine-producing regions, Rioja is famous for its food, which, like its wine, is full-bodied. The cooking is based on the produce of the land, especially the sweet red peppers, and the vegetables in general are exceptional.

Navarra

This region of Spain includes forests, torrential rivers, and the green mountain meadows of the Pyrenees Mountains. Ernest Hemingway immortalized Navarra in *The Sun Also Rises* with his description of the running of the bulls in Pamplona. Cattle and sheep are abundant, and Navarra is famous for lamb, trout, game, and white asparagus.

Aragón

The past is still a part of the present in the ancient kingdom of Aragón. This is the land of Roman legions, kings and queens, Moors and Christians, convents and castles. The landscape has hardly changed since the Middle Ages, with shepherds in the fields and medieval towns hanging onto cliffs. The food here is plain and simple: lamb roasted on a wood fire, shepherds' stews, and ham and sausages that are cured as they have been for centuries. This is food without adornment—just good-quality fruits, vegetables, lamb, and game.

Castilla-León

This is the land of castles in Spain and the birthplace of kings, saints, and great warriors. The provinces of this region share a treasure of Spanish monuments, landmarks, and art and are also the home of Castilian, the classic Spanish language. The land is austere and the climate quite harsh, with fierce winters and seeringly hot summers. There are vast wheatfields that produce most of the country's grain. Castilla-León is also a sportsman's paradise with all kinds of game. The gastronomic specialties include roast suckling pig, roast baby lamb, and excellent chorizo.

La Mancha

The name *La Mancha* comes from the Arabic *al manchara*, meaning "dry, flat land." The region's agriculture is typical of an extremely dry climate: grains, olives, and grapes are grown here. La Mancha is also the source of Spain's most famous cheese, Manchego, which is traditionally ewe's milk cheese cured in oil but may also be sold fresh or aged. The region produces a great amount of wine and the world's best saffron. The cooking is sturdy and simple with an emphasis on soups and stews.

Catalunya

Once a kingdom that extended into France, Catalunya (or in English, Catalonia) today is an autonomous region with its own language and dynamic traditions. As a seafaring nation, it gathered an eclectic mix of foods from all over the world. There are pastas from Italy, rice dishes from Valencia, hearty country food from neighboring Aragón, and saffron fish soups from Provence. Catalunya assimilated all these and superimposed its own culinary style. The use of honey, fruits, and nuts in main-course dishes traces its origin to medieval times, while chocolate, tomatoes, and peppers came with the discovery of the New World. Today the region is noted for excellent fish, vegetables and fruits, pasta, first-rate virgin olive oils, and fine wines.

Madrid

Madrid was made Spain's capital in the early 1600s, and it thus became the home of royalty and aristocracy. The preferences of imported chefs from Italy and France and the importance of the city's restaurants influenced the cooking of Madrid. People from all over Spain brought their provincial style of cooking with them when they moved to the city seeking work, culture, and trade. Today Madrid is famous for seafood as fresh as any coastal city's, fresh produce from the country, roasts of baby lamb and suckling pig, stews of chick peas or beans, chorizo, and *serrano* ham.

Extremadura

This harsh land along the Portuguese border was the home of the conquistadors. It is a broad plain with forests of cork oaks and chestnuts, olives, and vineyards. The countryside is devoted to grazing livestock, and the region is noted for lamb, kid, game, and *serrano* ham. The food is simple and hearty among the shepherds and peasants, while the region's monasteries have a tradition of good eating that includes such dishes as pheasant and partridge that have been marinated in port and stuffed with a duck liver and truffle pâté.

El Levante

The east of Spain is known as the land of paella, Spain's great rice dish. Water is abundant in the low coastal regions, and rice has been the staple crop since the Moors introduced it. The gentle climate and sandy beaches of the region have also made it an attraction for tourists. Gastronomically the region is noted for its seafood and produce. Valencia oranges, peaches, apricots, melons, grapes, pears, capers, onions, mushrooms, tomatoes, lettuce, and dates are grown here.

Andalucía

This is the romantic Spain of flamenco, Gypsies, white villages, flowered patios, Moorish palaces, golden beaches, and blue waters. This extensive region includes Spain's highest mountains—the snow-capped Sierra Nevada above Granada— the beaches of the Costa del Sol, and the sherry bodegas of Jerez. The Moorish influence on the food in Andalucía is very strong. Tapas are a way of life here, and specialties include seafood, gazpacho, desserts based on honey and almonds, and sauces seasoned with the saffron, coriander, and cumin introduced by the Arabs.

Balearic Islands

The Balearic Islands have received many influences because of their geographic position. Mallorca isn't quite Spanish, but rather part ancient myth and part fantasy for the tourist industry. Hercules discovered the golden apples in Mallorca, and Romans, Moors, and Barbary pirates are also part of the islands' history. The language is similar to that of Catalunya, as is the cuisine, but Italian and French influences are also strong. Menorca was ruled by the British for almost eighty years and as a result its specialties include English gin, English pudding and jams, stuffed turkey, and macaroni with gravy.

Canary Islands

These seven volcanic islands are located more than five hundred miles from mainland Spain and only seventy miles from the coast of northwest Africa. They are said to be part of the lost continent of Atlantis. Spaniards took over the islands in the fifteenth century, when the conquistadors made them the starting point for their voyages to the New World. The Canary Islands have a very mild climate that is perfect for bananas, mangoes, guavas, papayas, loquats, avocados, melons, and yams. The seafood is excellent, and some dishes use foods such as black beans, squash, and corn, brought back from the New World by the Spanish.

Bay Wolf Restaurant

Oakland, California

Bay Wolf Restaurant has been serving a blend of traditional French and Italian based dishes with a California influence since 1975 when owners Michael Wild and Larry Goldman transformed a vacant house into an art-filled restaurant. The menu changes every two weeks and consists of a selection of appetizers and five innovative entrées. The restaurant also features Spanish food and serves tapas such as the following ones prepared for *Menus and Music*. Tapas, a centuries-old tradition in Spain, may be almost any dish served in small portions and eaten as an appetizer or as a light meal.

MENU

Duck Turnovers

Ribbon Tarts

Endives Stuffed with Red Peppers and Almonds

Fried Fish

Lamb and Tongue Brochettes

Artichoke Aïoli and Romesco Sauce

Crab and Chorizo Omelet

Potatoes Stuffed with Cod Salad

Shrimp Tartlets

Duck Turnovers
Empanadillas de Pato

Empanadillas de pato are turnovers of duck, spinach, and pine nuts served with a spiced pear sauce.

PEAR SAUCE

2 pounds pears, peeled, cored, and quartered

1 cup dry sherry

1 cup sherry wine vinegar

1 cinnamon stick

6 garlic cloves, sliced

3 shallots, sliced

1 tablespoon minced fresh ginger

1 teaspoon dried red chili flakes

FILLING

2 bunches spinach, stemmed

1 red onion, cut into small dice

3 garlic cloves, minced

1 red bell pepper, cored, seeded, and cut into small dice

1/4 cup extra-virgin Spanish olive oil

1/2 cup pine nuts

1/4 cup currants

1 cup dry sherry

2 cups diced cooked duck meat

2 pounds fresh or thawed frozen puff pastry

1 egg beaten with 2 tablespoons water

To make the pear sauce: Combine all the sauce ingredients in a nonaluminum saucepan. Simmer until the pears are tender, 30 to 45 minutes. Remove the cinnamon stick and purée the mixture in a blender or food processor until smooth. Set aside.

To make the filling: Wash the spinach well but do not dry it. In a large saucepan, place the spinach over medium heat, cover, and cook for 2 to 3 minutes, or just until wilted. Let cool, then divide into small handfuls and squeeze each one in your hand to release as much moisture as possible. Mince the spinach and set it aside. In a sauté pan or skillet, sauté the onion, garlic, and red pepper in the olive oil until the onion is translucent, about 5 minutes. Add the pine nuts and sauté for 1 minute. Add the currants and sherry and cook over medium heat until the liquid has evaporated; let cool. Add the duck meat and spinach and correct the seasoning.

Preheat the oven to 450°F. Roll out the puff pastry to a thickness of ⅛ inch and cut it into 3-inch squares. Place 1 tablespoon filling in the center of each square and fold over on the diagonal. Seal with a few drops of water, brush with the egg-water glaze, and chill. Bake in the preheated oven for 10 minutes, then turn the oven down to 350°F and bake for 10 minutes longer, or until golden brown. Serve at once, with the pear sauce on the side.

Makes 15 to 25 tapas

Ribbon Tarts

B a n d a s

*Bandas are colorful tarts layered with roasted
peppers, anchovies, and olives.*

1 pound fresh or thawed frozen puff pastry

4 garlic cloves, minced

2 tablespoons extra-virgin Spanish olive oil

6 red and yellow bell peppers, roasted, cored, seeded,
and cut into strips (page 185)

4 ounces mild fresh goat cheese at room temperature (optional)

2 ounces salt-packed Spanish anchovies, soaked in
cold water for 15 minutes and drained

2 cups green and black olives, pitted and chopped

Roll the puff pastry into 2 rectangles ⅛ inch thick, 8 inches wide, and about
16 inches long. Cut into two 4-inch pieces. Cut off a ½-inch band on all 4
sides of both pieces. Brush cold water on the edges of the strips and lay the
bands of dough along the edges to make the rims of the tarts; press to seal
the rims. Prick the centers with a fork and chill.

Preheat the oven to 450°F. In a sauté pan or skillet, sauté the garlic in the
olive oil for 2 or 3 minutes. Toss the peppers with the garlic and set aside.
Spread a layer of goat cheese over the pastry, if you like. Arrange the
peppers on the tart shells in long ribbons, alternating colors. Garnish with
anchovies and olives. Bake for 15 minutes. Turn the oven down to 375°F and
bake 15 minutes longer, or until the pastry is puffed and golden. Slice each
tart into fifteen 1-inch pieces and serve them hot or cool.

Makes 30 tapas

Endives Stuffed with Red Peppers and Almonds
Endibias Rellenas

3 large red Anaheim chilies, or 3 red bell peppers and
1 jalapeño chili, cored, seeded, and chopped

1 red onion, sliced

6 garlic cloves, minced

½ cup extra-virgin Spanish olive oil

½ cup sherry vinegar or red wine vinegar

1 cup almonds, lightly toasted (page 190)

Salt to taste

4 to 6 endives

Chopped fresh chives for garnish

In a sauté pan or skillet, sauté the chilies, peppers, onion, and garlic in the olive oil until the onion is translucent, about 5 minutes. Add the vinegar and cook over medium heat until the liquid evaporates. Grind the almonds in a blender or a food processor. Add the vegetables and purée to a thick paste; add salt to taste. Separate the endives into leaves and spread the paste on the leaves. Garnish with chives.

Makes about 40 tapas

Fried Fish

P e s c a d o s   F r i t o s

*Pescados fritos are deep-fried small fish
in a cornmeal-beer batter.*

B A T T E R

1 cup unbleached all-purpose flour

1 cup stone-ground cornmeal

3 cups beer

1 tablespoon salt

1 teaspoon Tabasco sauce

Oil for deep-frying*

2 to 3 pounds any small fish (fresh anchovies, whitebait,
squid, shrimp, or finger-sized slices of sea bass,
snapper, or other firm white-fleshed fish)

In a large bowl, whisk together all the ingredients for the batter. Chill for 30 minutes. The batter should be just thick enough to coat the fish.

In a deep, heavy pot or deep-fryer pour oil to a depth of 3 to 4 inches. Heat the oil to 340°F, or until it will crisp a bread cube in 30 to 40 seconds. Dip the fish into the batter and fry in small batches until crisp. Drain on paper towels and serve hot.

Makes about 40 tapas

* Preferably a mix of half olive oil and half peanut oil, although you must be careful not to let the oil overheat.

Lamb and Tongue Brochettes
Cordero y Lengua Brochetas

MARINADE

1 cup olive oil

½ cup dry red wine

2 tablespoons paprika

6 garlic cloves, minced

2 pounds lamb from loin or leg, trimmed of fat and cut into 1-inch cubes

2 pounds lamb or veal tongue, poached, peeled, and cut into 1-inch cubes

2 red bell peppers, cored, seeded, and cut into 1-inch squares

2 bunches green onions, cut into 1-inch lengths

In a medium bowl, mix together all the marinade ingredients. Place the lamb in a nonaluminum container, pour the marinade over, and marinate at room temperature for 1 hour. If you are using bamboo skewers, place them in water to soak.

Light a fire in a charcoal grill or preheat the broiler. Put 1 cube of lamb and 1 piece of tongue on each of 30 to 40 skewers, alternating with pepper and onion. Grill or broil for 3 to 4 minutes on each side, or until medium rare, and serve immediately.

Makes 30 to 40 tapas

Artichoke Aïoli
Alioli de Alcachofa

Artichoke alioli, a Catalán version of aïoli, can be used as a dipping sauce for fried fish, vegetables, and the brochetas on the preceding page. Prepare this sauce the day before serving to allow the flavors to mellow and mingle.

3 large artichokes

½ lemon

¼ cup distilled white vinegar

12 garlic cloves

1½ teaspoons salt

3 egg yolks

2 cups extra-virgin olive oil, preferably Spanish

¼ cup fresh lemon juice

Cut off the base of the artichokes and break off all the leaves up to the top third; cut off the top with a sharp knife. Cut out the choke with a teaspoon. Rub all over with the lemon. Add the vinegar to a large pot of boiling salted water and cook the artichoke hearts until tender, about 30 minutes.

Purée the artichoke hearts in a blender or a food processor and set aside. In a large bowl, mash the garlic and salt together with a pestle or the back of a spoon. Whisk in the egg yolks, then whisk in the olive oil drop by drop until the sauce is emulsified; gradually whisk in the rest of the oil in a thin stream. Stir in the lemon juice and the artichoke purée. Correct the seasoning.

Makes about 3 cups

Romesco Sauce

Salsa Romesco

This famous Catalán sauce is used as a dipping sauce for fried fish, vegetables, and broiled or grilled meats. Make the sauce several hours before serving to allow the flavors to develop.

6 dried New Mexico or other large mild dried red chilies

1½ cups water

1 cup red wine vinegar

8 garlic cloves

1½ teaspoons salt

½ cup slivered blanched almonds, toasted (page 190)

1 cup fresh bread crumbs

1½ cups extra-virgin olive oil, preferably Spanish

3 tomatoes, peeled and seeded (page 189)

In a medium saucepan, simmer the chilies in the water and vinegar until softened. Drain the chilies, reserving the water, and remove the seeds and stems. Purée the chilies with a little of the soaking water in a blender or a food processor. In a mortar, grind the garlic and salt together with a pestle. Add the almonds and garlic-salt to the chilies; purée to a paste.

In a sauté pan or skillet, fry the bread crumbs in ½ cup of the olive oil. Add to the blender along with the tomatoes; purée. With the motor running, add the remaining 1 cup of the olive oil slowly through the top of the blender. The sauce will emulsify and should be fairly thick. Season with salt and pepper.

Makes about 3 cups

Crab and Chorizo Omelet

Tortilla de Cangrejo

This savory omelet is delicious hot, warm, or cold.

2 onions, cut into small dice

4 garlic cloves, minced

8 ounces Spanish chorizo or Cajun andouille
sausage, cut into small dice

½ cup extra-virgin olive oil, preferably Spanish

2 tomatoes, peeled, seeded, and chopped (page 189)

9 eggs

8 ounces fresh or thawed and drained frozen crab meat

In a sauté pan or skillet, sauté the onions, garlic, and sausage in 2 tablespoons of the olive oil until the onions are translucent, about 5 minutes. Add the tomatoes and cook for about 3 minutes over medium heat until thick; let cool. In a large bowl, beat the eggs and mix in the crab and sausage-tomato mixture.

Heat an 8-inch sauté pan or skillet until very hot. Add 2 tablespoons of the olive oil and pour in one third of the egg mixture. Lower the heat and cook until browned on the bottom. Turn the omelet over and cook until browned on the other side. Remove to a platter. Repeat with the other 2 batches. Cut the omelets into cubes and serve at room temperature.

Makes about 40 tapas

Potatoes Stuffed with Cod Salad
P a t a t a s R e l l e n a s c o n B a c a l a o

*Although it is not a Mediterranean fish, the Spanish love
dried salt cod. Aficionados will tell you it is one of the
great acquired tastes, like caviar or truffles.*

COD SALAD

1 pound salt cod, soaked overnight and drained

3 garlic cloves

¼ cup fresh lemon juice

½ cup extra-virgin olive oil, preferably Spanish

2 red bell peppers, cored, seeded, and minced

1 bunch green onions, minced

20 small new white or red potatoes, halved

20 cherry tomatoes, halved

To make the cod salad: Preheat the oven to 400°F. Place the salt cod in a
large pot, add water to cover, and bring to a boil. Remove from heat, drain,
and shred. Mix the fish with the remaining salad ingredients and set aside.

Place the potatoes in a baking dish where they will have plenty of room. Add
the olive oil and turn to coat the potatoes well. Roast the potatoes, turning
occasionally, until tender and crisp, about 25 minutes. Hollow out the
centers and fill with the salad. Top with a cherry tomato half. Serve hot or at
room temperature.

Makes 40 tapas

Shrimp Tartlets

Tartaletas de Gamba

PÂTÉ À CHOUX

1½ cups water

½ cup (1 stick) butter

Salt and freshly ground pepper to taste

1½ cups unbleached all-purpose flour

6 eggs

1 cup freshly grated Parmesan cheese

FILLING

1 bunch dandelion greens, minced

4 ounces Westphalian ham or prosciutto, minced

6 garlic cloves, minced

1 large onion, cut into small dice

½ cup extra-virgin Spanish olive oil, preferably Spanish

2 pounds medium shrimp, shelled

2 egg whites, slightly beaten

2 eggs, beaten

To make the pâté à choux: Preheat the oven to 425°F. Place the water in a heavy, medium saucepan and bring it to a boil; add the butter and cook until melted. Add salt and pepper. Off heat, pour in all the flour and stir quickly to blend. Over medium-high heat, cook and stir the mixture until it leaves the side of the pan. Remove from heat. Break 1 egg into the pan and stir it rapidly into the mixture. Repeat one by one with the remaining eggs, then rapidly stir in the Parmesan cheese.

To make the filling: In a sauté pan or skillet, sauté the greens, ham, garlic, and onion in the olive oil until the onion is translucent, about 5 minutes. Let cool. Cut the shrimp into 1/8-inch pieces and coat with the egg whites. Toss with the greens mixture and set aside.

Place the pâté in a pastry bag with a plain tip and pipe in 2-inch rounds on buttered baking sheets. Press a tablespoonful of filling in the center of each tart. Brush the tops with the beaten eggs. Bake for 15 minutes, or until puffed and golden brown. Serve immediately.

Makes about 30 tapas

Cafe Ba-Ba-Reeba!

Chicago, Illinois

This festive Chicago restaurant serves over six thousand tapas every Saturday night. Paella and regional specialties also are served in the restaurant's bright and lively dining rooms, and drinks are enjoyed at the traditional Spanish bar.

MENU

Baby Shrimp and Scallops

Cold Grilled Swordfish

Grilled Beef Tenderloin with Blue Cheese and Garlic Potato Chips

Baby Shrimp and Scallops

Salpicón Blanco

*Serve this shellfish salad as a tapa or first course and be sure
to provide crusty bread to soak up the sauce.*

1 gallon water

1 bay leaf

2 peppercorns

2 lemons

8 ounces baby shrimp

1 pound bay scallops

1 Roma (plum) tomato, diced

1 small red bell pepper, cored, seeded, and diced

1 small green bell pepper, cored, seeded, and diced

1 tablespoon capers, drained

2 tablespoons minced fresh cilantro

2 tablespoons olive oil

Tabasco sauce, salt, and freshly ground pepper to taste

In a large stockpot over medium-high heat, place the water, bay leaf,
peppercorns, and the juice of 1 lemon. Bring the water to a simmer and add
the shrimp and scallops. Simmer the shellfish until just cooked through,
about 4 to 5 minutes; drain.

In a medium bowl, mix together the tomato, peppers, lemon juice from the
remaining lemon, capers, cilantro, and olive oil. Add the shrimp and scallops
and refrigerate until chilled. Season with Tabasco, salt, and pepper.

Makes 4 servings

Cold Grilled Swordfish
Pez Espada a la Parrilla

SAUCE

1/2 red onion

1/2 teaspoon salt

1/2 tablespoon chopped fresh oregano

1/2 cup olive oil

1/3 cup sherry vinegar

1/4 cup diced red bell pepper

1 large tomato, diced

Salt to taste

Two 2-ounce swordfish fillets

To make the sauce: Slice the onion into thin half circles. In a medium bowl, mix together all the remaining sauce ingredients. Cover and refrigerate until needed.

Light a fire in a charcoal grill. When the coals are hot, grill the swordfish for 3 to 4 minutes on each side, or until just opaque throughout. Spoon the sauce on top of the fish and refrigerate until chilled.

Makes 2 servings

Grilled Beef Tenderloin with Blue Cheese and Garlic Potato Chips

Solomillo con Cabrales
con Papas Ajo

Spain produces excellent blue-veined cheeses in the northern mountains of the country.

BLUE CHEESE TOPPING

1/4 cup fresh white bread crumbs

4 ounces blue cheese, preferably Spanish*

2 tablespoons butter

Two 3 1/2 -ounce beef tenderloin medallions

Garlic Potato Chips (recipe follows)

To make the blue cheese topping: In a blender or food processor, purée all the topping ingredients. Place in a small bowl, cover, and chill.

Light a fire in a charcoal grill. When the coals are hot, grill the beef medallions for 3 to 4 minutes on each side for medium rare. Meanwhile, preheat the broiler. Remove the meat from the grill and pack some of the blue cheese mixture on top of each medallion. Place the medallions under the broiler until the cheese just melts. Serve immediately with the garlic potato chips.

Makes 2 servings

* Spanish blue cheese is available from La Española in Lomita, California. Telephone 310-539-0455, or fax 310-539-5989.

GARLIC POTATO CHIPS

2 Idaho potatoes

4 tablespoons (1/2 stick) butter

2 tablespoons minced garlic

Vegetable oil for deep-frying

Salt to taste

Peel and slice the potatoes into thin rounds, placing them in a bowl of cold water to prevent discoloration. Place the oil to a depth of 2 inches in a large, heavy pot or deep-fryer. Heat the oil over high heat until it sizzles when a drop of water is sprinkled into it. Drain the potatoes and pat them dry on paper towels. Lower heat to medium and fry the potato slices in small batches. Drain on paper towels.

In a skillet or sauté pan over low heat, melt the butter and sauté the garlic. Once the garlic starts to bubble, pour it over the chips. Add salt and serve at once.

Makes 2 servings

Cafe Seville

Antonio and Jose Servan have recreated the feeling of a neighborhood cafe in Seville in their cozy dining room in South Florida. The menu of this award-winning restaurant has an abundance of local seafood prepared in the Spanish style, and the desserts also are classically Spanish.

MENU

Garlic Shrimp

Chilled Tomato Soup

Rabbit Stew

Baked Snapper Costa Brava

Catalán Custard

Garlic Shrimp
G a m b a s   a l   A j i l l o

A delicious appetizer, garlic shrimp is quick and easy to prepare.

2 tablespoons olive oil

12 ounces medium shrimp, shelled

4 garlic cloves, minced

Pinch of dried red pepper flakes

2 teaspoons beef or veal broth

2 teaspoons fresh lemon juice

2 teaspoons dry sherry

2 teaspoons minced fresh parsley

Salt and white pepper to taste

In a sauté pan or skillet over medium-high heat, heat the olive oil and sauté the shrimp for 2 minutes. Add all of the remaining ingredients. Sauté 2 minutes more or until the shrimp are just evenly pink and slightly curled. Serve immediately, preferably in a clay casserole.

Makes 6 servings

Chilled Tomato Soup

Gazpacho Andaluz

This famous chilled soup originated in Andalusía and is extremely refreshing during hot weather.

1½ pounds ripe tomatoes, chopped

1 medium green bell pepper, cored, seeded, and chopped

1 small onion, chopped

1 small cucumber, peeled and chopped

½ cup olive oil

2 stale French bread rolls, broken into pieces

1 cup tomato juice

¼ cup red wine vinegar

¼ teaspoon dried thyme

1 garlic clove, chopped

1 teaspoon salt

White pepper to taste

2 tablespoons each diced cucumber, green pepper,
onion, and croutons for garnish

In a large nonaluminum bowl, place all the ingredients except the salt, pepper, and garnish; add water to cover and refrigerate overnight. In a blender or food processor, purée the chilled mixture. Strain, add salt and pepper, and chill. Pass the garnishes in small bowls with the chilled soup.

Makes 6 to 8 servings

Note: Gazpacho keeps well in the refrigerator for several days.

Rabbit Stew

Conejo en Su Salsa

*Rabbit is popular in Spain, and its meat
is flavorful, tender, and low in fat.*

6 tablespoons olive oil

Two 1½-pound rabbits, cut into serving pieces

1 onion, chopped

2 garlic cloves, minced

1 bay leaf

2 tablespoons minced fresh parsley

2 tablespoons salt

2 tablespoons white pepper

2 to 3 cups dry white wine

2 to 3 cups water

In a deep, heavy pot, heat the olive oil and add all the ingredients except the wine and water. Add equal amounts of wine and water until until the rabbit pieces are completely submerged. Bring to a boil, then reduce heat to low. Simmer for 1½ hours, or until very tender. Serve a bowl of the cooking broth alongside the rabbit.

Makes 4 servings

Baked Snapper Costa Brava

1 to 1½ pounds snapper, or rockfish fillets

Flour for dredging

Salt to taste

¼ cup olive oil

2 tablespoons unsalted butter, cut into pieces

½ tomato, diced

2 teaspoons minced green onions

2 tablespoons dry sherry

½ cup dry white wine

Preheat the oven to 450°F. Dredge the fish fillets in flour and season with salt. In an ovenproof sauté pan or skillet, heat the olive oil over medium-high heat. Add the fish fillets, skin-side up, and fry until golden. Turn the fillets over and top with the remaining ingredients.

Place the skillet in the preheated oven and bake for 10 minutes. Remove the fish to a platter and top with the pan sauce. Serve immediately.

Makes 2 servings

Catalán Custard

Crema Catalana

*This delicious lemon and cinnamon-flavored custard is covered
with a caramelized sugar crust.*

4 whole eggs

1/2 cup unbleached all-purpose flour

4 cups milk

2/3 cup granulated sugar

1 cinnamon stick

Zest of 1/2 lemon

1/4 teaspoon vanilla extract

1/3 cup packed light brown sugar

Ground cinnamon to taste

In a small bowl, beat the eggs with the flour until perfectly smooth. In a saucepan over medium heat, bring the milk just to a boil with the sugar, cinnamon stick, lemon zest, and vanilla extract. Remove the cinnamon stick with a slotted spoon. Slowly add the egg-flour mixture, stirring constantly, until the custard is thick and smooth. Allow to just reach the boiling point and then immediately remove it from heat. Strain through a fine sieve, pour into 6 individual clay or ovenproof dishes, and refrigerate until well chilled.

To serve, preheat the broiler. Sieve brown sugar evenly over the top of each custard and sprinkle with cinnamon. Place under the broiler until the sugar caramelizes, 2 to 3 minutes. Let cool.

Makes 6 servings

Cafe TuTu Tango

Miami, Florida

Cafe Tu Tu Tango in Miami's Coconut Grove looks like an artist's loft in Barcelona. The dining area is plentifully supplied with artists' accoutrements, including tableware in a brush pot at each place setting. Live artists painting at easels, tango and flamenco dancers, and fire eaters are often part of the scene. The kitchen presents dishes that are both inventive and satisfying.

MENU

Gazpacho Salad

Drunken Shrimp with Sun-dried Tomato Aïoli

Grilled Beef Tenderloin with Red Onion Marmalade

Chocolate Plantain Mousse

Gazpacho Salad

TOMATO VINAIGRETTE

1 cup lightly packed fresh basil leaves, chopped

2 tablespoons balsamic vinegar

1 1/2 teaspoons Dijon mustard

Salt and freshly ground pepper to taste

1 Roma (plum) tomato, peeled and seeded, and diced (page 189)

1 teaspoon minced garlic

1 teaspoon minced shallots

1/3 cup olive oil

SALAD

2 Roma (plum) tomatoes, seeded and cut into 1/4-inch dice

1 cucumber, peeled, seeded, and cut into 1/4-inch dice

1 red bell pepper, cored, seeded, and diced

1 onion, diced

6 ounces (6 cups) mixed greens (baby oakleaf,
Bibb, romaine, frisée), finely chopped

Croûtons (page 181), optional

To make the vinaigrette: In a medium bowl, whisk together all of the ingredients except the olive oil. Add the olive oil slowly in a steady stream, whisking the entire time.

To make the salad : In a large bowl, toss together all the salad ingredients except the croûtons. Let sit for 3 to 4 minutes so the vegetables can absorb the tomato vinaigrette. Mound the salad in the center of 4 serving plates and garnish with croûtons, if desired.

Makes 4 servings

Drunken Shrimp with Sun-dried Tomato Aïoli

Marinated shrimp with a fast version of aïoli that is almost as good as the handmade kind and takes only one fourth the effort and time.

SUN-DRIED TOMATO AIOLI

1 cup good-quality mayonnaise

1/4 cup fresh lemon juice

4 crushed garlic cloves

1/4 cup sun-dried tomatoes

1 tablespoon Dijon mustard

3/4 cup tequila

3/4 cup fresh lime juice

1/4 cup olive oil

2 tablespoons minced garlic cloves

2 tablespoons minced shallots

1 pound jumbo shrimp, shelled and deveined

To make the aïoli: In a blender or food processor, process all the ingredients until smooth. Chill.

In a medium nonaluminum bowl, combine the tequila, lime juice, olive oil, garlic, and shallots. Add the shrimp, cover, and marinate in the refrigerator for 2 to 3 hours. Just before serving, drain the shrimp and serve with sun-dried tomato aïoli.

Makes 4 servings

Grilled Beef Tenderloin with Red Onion Marmalade

HORSERADISH SOUR CREAM

1/4 cup prepared grated horseradish, drained

1/4 cup sour cream

1 teaspoon Worcestershire sauce

Salt and freshly ground pepper to taste

1 pound beef tenderloin, cut into 1-inch cubes

6 ounces cracked black peppercorns

Red Onion Marmalade (recipe follows)

To make the sour cream: In a small bowl, stir together all the ingredients and chill in the refrigerator until serving.

Light a fire in a charcoal grill or preheat a broiler. Soak 6 bamboo skewers in water to cover for 15 to 30 minutes. Skewer 3 pieces of beef on each bamboo skewer and roll them in the cracked black peppercorns. Grill over hot coals or under the broiler for 3 to 4 minutes on each side for medium rare.

Pool the horseradish sour cream on 2 serving plates and arrange 3 skewers on top of the sauce on each plate. Garnish with the red onion marmalade.

Makes 2 servings

RED ONION MARMALADE

2 tablespoons olive oil

1 red onion, sliced thin

1/4 cup Burgundy or other dry red wine

1/4 cup cranberry juice

In a heavy sauté pan or skillet over low heat, heat the olive oil and sauté the onions until they begin to caramelize, stirring occasionally; this may take up to 30 minutes. Pour the red wine into the pan and stir to dislodge any browned bits on the bottom of the pan. Add the cranberry juice, increase the heat to high, and cook until three fourths of the liquid has evaporated. Let cool before serving.

Makes 2 servings

Chocolate Plantain Mousse

*Plantains or bananas give this chocolate mousse
an unusual tropical flavor.*

8 ounces semisweet chocolate

2 egg yolks

3/4 cup sugar

2 cups heavy (whipping) cream

2 small ripe plantains (see Note) or bananas

2 tablespoons banana liqueur (optional)

2 tablespoons Cointreau

In a double boiler over simmering water, melt the chocolate. In a medium bowl, whip the egg yolks and 1/2 cup of the sugar together until thick and pale.

In a deep bowl, whip the cream and remaining 1/4 cup sugar until stiff peaks form. Mash the plantains or bananas with a fork or purée in a blender until smooth.

Slowly whisk the warm chocolate into the yolk-sugar mixture. Blend in the plantain or banana purée. Gently fold in the whipped cream, optional liqueur, and Cointreau. Spoon into 6 goblets or wineglasses and chill in the refrigerator until serving.

Makes 6 to 8 servings

Note: The skin of plantains is black when they are fully ripened.

Columbia Restaurant

Tampa, Florida

The Columbia Restaurant, America's oldest Spanish restaurant, was established in 1905 by Casimiro Hernandez. Sr. Adela Gonzmart, a Juilliard-trained pianist and grandaughter of the restaurant's founder, and her husband Cesar, a concert violinist, took over the family business in the 1950s and it has expanded ever since. Today, the restaurant has eleven dining rooms and serves over 1.5 million people each year. The Columbia features a live orchestra and flamenco shows nightly.

MENU

1905 Salad

Snapper Alicante

Spanish Bean Soup

Filet Steak Columbia

Flan

1905 Salad

*This popular Columbia salad is named for the
year the restaurant was founded.*

GARLIC VINAIGRETTE

1/4 cup white wine vinegar

1 cup olive oil

8 garlic cloves, minced

1 teaspoon minced fresh oregano

2 teaspoons Worcestershire sauce

Salt and pepper to taste

1 head iceburg lettuce

4 tomatoes, diced

6 ounces Swiss cheese, julienned (about 1 1/2 cups)

6 ounces ham, julienned (about 1 1/2 cups)

2/3 cup pitted olives, preferably Spanish

1 to 2 teaspoons grated romano cheese

Juice of 1 lemon

In a small bowl, whisk all the vinaigrette ingredients together; set aside.

Chop the lettuce and place in a large bowl. Add the tomatoes, Swiss cheese, ham, and Spanish olives. Pour the garlic vinaigrette over and add the romano cheese and lemon juice. Toss all the ingredients together and serve the salad on chilled plates.

Makes 4 servings

Snapper Alicante

*This specialty of the Columbia Restaurant was created by
Casimiro Hernandez, Jr., son of the restaurant's founder.*

1 onion, cut into rounds

1 pound red snapper or rockfish fillets

1/4 cup olive oil

1/2 cup brown sauce (page 178)

1/2 teaspoon salt

White pepper to taste

1/2 green bell pepper, cored, seeded, and cut into rings

12 sliced almonds, toasted (page 190)

1/4 cup dry white wine

4 slices Fried Eggplant (recipe follows)

4 Shrimp Supreme (recipe follows)

Preheat the oven to 350°F. In an ovenproof casserole, preferably made of
clay, place the sliced onions and top with the fish fillets. Spoon the olive oil
and brown sauce over the fish and season with salt and pepper. Place a few
green pepper rings on top of the fish fillets and sprinkle with the sliced
almonds. Bake, uncovered, for 25 minutes, or until the fish is opaque
throughout. Remove from the oven and sprinkle with the white wine.

Arrange the fish on serving plates and garnish with the fried eggplant and
shrimp.

Makes 2 servings

FRIED EGGPLANT

1 globe eggplant

Salt for sprinkling

Bread crumbs for dredging

3 tablespoons olive oil

Peel and slice the eggplant into 1/2-inch-thick slices. Layer the slices in a collander, sprinkle liberally with salt, and let drain for 1 hour. Rinse the eggplant under running water, drain, and pat dry. Dredge the slices in flour.

In a sauté pan or skillet over medium-high heat, heat the olive oil and sauté the eggplant slices until both sides are golden. Drain on paper towels, season with salt, and serve hot.

Makes 2 servings

SHRIMP SUPREME

4 large shrimp, shelled and deveined

Juice of 1 lemon

Salt and freshly ground pepper to taste

2 bacon strips

1 egg, beaten with 1/4 cup milk

Flour for dredging

Olive oil for deep-frying

In a small nonaluminum bowl, combine the shrimp, lemon juice, salt, and pepper. Cover and marinate in the refrigerator for several hours.

Cut the bacon strips in half lengthwise. Wrap a slice around each shrimp and skewer in place with a toothpick. Dip the shrimp in the beaten egg and milk, then dredge in the flour.

Into a deep, heavy skillet pour olive oil to a depth of 1 inch. Heat the olive oil over medium-high heat until the oil sizzles when a drop of water is sprinkled on it. Fry the shrimp until golden, about 3 minutes. Remove with a slotted spoon and drain on paper towels.

Makes 4 servings

Spanish Bean Soup

*This soup is popular in the winter. Serve with a salad
and crusty bread for a light supper.*

8 ounces dried garbanzo beans

1 tablespoon salt

8 cups water

1 ham bone

1 beef bone

4 ounces salt pork

1 onion, finely chopped

2 potatoes, cut into quarters

1/4 teaspoon saffron threads

1/2 teaspoon paprika

1 chorizo sausage

Wash the garbanzos and soak them overnight in salted water to cover. Drain the beans and place them in a 4-quart soup kettle. Add the water and bones. Simmer over medium-low heat for 45 minutes, skimming any foam that rises to the top.

Cut the salt pork into thin strips and fry in a skillet over medium-low heat. Add the onion and cook until translucent, about 5 minutes. Add the salt pork and onion to the beans with the potatoes, saffron, paprika, and salt to taste. Simmer for 15 to 20 minutes, until the potatoes are tender. Slice the chorizo into thin rounds and add 5 minutes before removing the soup from heat.

Makes 4 servings

Filet Steak Columbia

Two 1-inch-thick filet mignon steaks

Salt and freshly ground pepper to taste

4 bacon strips

2 tablespoons olive oil

1 onion, chopped

1 green bell pepper, cored, seeded, and chopped

½ cup tomato sauce (page 188)

½ cup brown sauce (page 178)

½ cup dry red wine

Preheat the broiler. Season the steaks with salt and pepper and wrap each with 2 strips of bacon secured with toothpicks.

In a skillet or sauté pan over medium heat, heat the olive oil and sauté the onion until translucent, about 5 minutes. Add the green pepper and sauté for 5 minutes. Add the tomato sauce, brown sauce, and wine; reduce heat to low and simmer until slightly thickened, about 5 minutes.

Broil the steaks 3 to 4 minutes on each side for medium rare, or to the desired degree of doneness. Place the steaks on heated plates and pour the sauce over.

Makes 2 servings

Flan

*The Columbia Restaurant's rendition of Spain's
classic caramel-topped custard.*

1 cup plus 6 tablespoons sugar

4 cups whole milk

1/8 teaspoon salt

8 eggs

1 teaspoon vanilla extract

Preheat the oven to 300°F. In a small, heavy skillet over medium-high heat, melt 6 tablespoons of the sugar until it turns a light golden color. Immediately remove the pan from heat and pour the caramel into a 6-cup mold, tilting to coat the bottom of the mold.

In a medium saucepan over medium-high heat, combine the milk and salt and heat the milk until scalding. Remove from heat and stir in the remaining 1 cup sugar until it dissolves; set aside.

In a large bowl, beat the eggs until slightly foamy. Gradually add the hot milk and sugar mixture and stir in the vanilla. Strain through a fine sieve and pour into the caramel-coated mold. Place the mold in a shallow baking dish and fill the dish with water to halfway up the sides of the mold. Bake in the preheated oven for about 1 hour, or until a knife inserted in the center of the flan comes out clean. Remove from the oven and allow to cool to room temperature before inverting onto a serving platter.

Makes 6 to 8 servings

El Racó de Can Fabes

Sant Celoní, Spain

Chef-owner Santi Santamaria prepares imaginative Mediterranean cuisine based on local ingredients and Catalán ideas in a stone mansion in the foothills of the Montseny Mountains, about a thirty-minute drive northeast of Barcelona. The interior of the restaurant is rustic while the kitchen is state-of-the-art and enclosed by glass, allowing patrons to watch Chef Santamaria at work.

MENU

Prawns Marinated with Garden Herbs

Partridge Cooked in Two Ways

Truffle-flavored Custards

Prawns Marinated with Garden Herbs

Gambas Marinadas con Hierbas de Jardin

Serve these marinated prawns as a tapa or first course.

HERB VINAIGRETTE

1/4 cup champagne or sherry wine vinegar

3/4 cup olive oil

Minced fresh chives, parsley, chervil, and dill to taste

Salt and freshly ground pepper to taste

16 prawns, shelled and deveined

Salt and freshly ground pepper to taste

In a medium nonaluminum bowl, whisk together all the vinaigrette ingredients; set aside.

Flatten the prawns between 2 sheets of plastic wrap and pound firmly with the flat end of a meat pounder. Refrigerate until the prawns become firm, about 30 minutes. Place the prawns in the vinaigrette and marinate for 15 minutes. Season with salt and pepper and serve.

Makes 4 servings

Partridge Cooked in Two Ways
P e r d i z   e n   D o s   T i e m p o s

Partridge is the most popular game bird in Spain, and is almost an everyday dish for many rural families. Cornish game hens or squabs may be substituted if partridges are unavailable.

Six 1-pound partridges,
Cornish game hens or squabs, rinsed and patted dry

1/2 cup olive oil

2 onions, chopped

4 tomatoes, chopped

4 carrots, peeled and diced

4 garlic cloves, chopped

2 tablespoons gin

6 small potatoes, peeled and diced

2 zucchini, diced

2 tablespoons butter

1 parsley sprig, stemmed and chopped

3 tablespoons chopped blanched almonds

Salt and freshly ground pepper to taste

2 tablespoons butter, chopped into pieces

Minced fresh parsley for garnish

Cut off the thigh-leg sections of the birds. In a skillet over medium heat, heat 3 tablespoons of the olive oil and brown the legs on all sides. Remove the legs and set aside.

In a deep, heavy casserole over medium heat, heat 1/4 cup of the olive oil and sauté the onions, tomatoes, half of the carrots, and half of the garlic for 5 minutes. Place the legs on top of the bed of vegetables. Add enough water to barely cover the legs. Bring to a boil, then reduce heat to low. Cover and simmer gently for 1 1/2 hours, stirring occasionally. Remove from heat and let cool.

Preheat the oven to 400°F. Remove the bones from the breasts of the birds. Chop the bones into small pieces and place them in a roasting pan with the vegetables. Roast uncovered in the oven for 30 minutes, or until a deep brown. Remove from the oven and transfer the bones and vegetables to a stockpot. Pour the gin into the roasting pan and place the pan over medium heat. Stir to dislodge any browned bits from the bottom of the pan; set aside.

Add enough water to the stockpot to cover the bones and vegetables. Bring to a boil over high heat and skim the surface to remove any foam that rises to the top. Reduce the heat to low and simmer, uncovered, for 2 hours, adding water as needed to keep the solids covered. Strain through a sieve.

In a large saucepan, heat the strained stock until simmering. Add the remaining carrots and cook for 10 minutes. Add the potatoes and continue simmering for 10 more minutes. Add the zucchini and cook until it is just tender, about 10 minutes. Remove from heat.

In a heavy skillet, heat the butter with 1 tablespoon of the olive oil and sauté the breasts until just opaque throughout, about 3 minutes on each side. Slice the breast meat. Place the breast meat and legs in a casserole, cover, and place in a low oven until serving.

In a mortar or blender, crush the remaining garlic, parsley, and almonds together; add 1 tablespoonful of stock and stir to make a smooth paste. Return the stock and cooked vegetables to the heat and stir in the garlic-nut paste. Simmer for 10 minutes and remove from heat. Add salt and pepper. Strain the liquid through a sieve. Return the liquid to medium-high heat and whisk in the pieces of butter until emulsified.

Arrange the sliced breast meat and legs in the center of a large platter with the carrots, potatoes, and zucchini arranged around them. Spoon some of the sauce over and garnish with parsley. Serve, passing the remaining sauce.

Makes 6 to 8 servings

Truffle-flavored Custards
Royal a la Esencia de Trufas

*An utterly delicious rich custard to serve with roasted
meats or poultry. Truffles are found in the Catalunya and
Extremadura regions of Spain.*

2 cups half and half

4 large egg yolks

2 tablespoons butter, melted

Salt and freshly ground pepper to taste

5 egg whites

1 cup heavy (whipping) cream or half and half

1/3 cup truffle juice from can, plus some for garnish

Preheat the oven to 325°F. Lightly butter six 4-ounce ovenproof ramekins.
Place the 2 cups half and half in a blender; add the egg yolks, butter, and
salt and pepper. Turn the blender on only long enough to liquefy the
ingredients, about 5 seconds. (If the eggs are overblended, their binding
ability will be broken down.)

In a large bowl, whisk together the egg yolk mixture, egg whites, 1 cup
cream or half and half, and truffle juice until smooth. Divide the custard
mixture evenly among the ramekins and place them in a baking dish. Pour
in enough hot water to reach halfway up the sides of the ramekins and place
the dish on the middle rack of the oven. Reduce the oven heat to 300°F and
bake the custards for 45 to 60 minutes, or until a skewer inserted in the
middle of a custard comes out clean. Let cool.

Run a knife blade around the inside of each ramekin and invert each custard onto a plate. Just before serving, spoon a little truffle juice over each custard.

Makes 6 servings

Hacienda Na Xamena

San Miguel, Ibiza

Hacienda Na Xamena is situated on a secluded promontory overlooking the dramatic bay of Na Xamena on the magical island of Ibiza. The hotel's architecture is based on traditional Ibizan design, and it is the island's only five-star hotel. Here, you may sit under the stars and sip small glasses of *hierbas*, a local liqueur, and enjoy authentic Roman or Carthaginian cuisine or the chef's *dégustation*, or tasting, menu.

M E N U

Red Mullet and Prawn Salad

Garlic-glazed Fillets of Sole with Red Pepper Sauce

Asparagus with Almond Sauce

Squab with Dates

Ibizan Cheese Tart

Red Mullet and Prawn Salad

Ensalada Templada
de Salmonetes y Longostinos

*Salads are especially popular in countries with hot climates,
and Spain is no exception. Cooked fish and shellfish are favorite
ingredients on top of a bed of greens with vinaigrette.*

VINAIGRETTE

1 cup olive oil

1/4 cup sherry or red wine vinegar

1 teaspoon Dijon mustard

16 prawns, shelled and deveined

Eight 3-ounce red mullet, mackerel, or pompano fillets, or
four 6-ounce firm white-fleshed fish fillets cut in half

Salt to taste

8 ounces mixed salad greens such as baby lettuces,
watercress, chicory, and endive

1 teaspoon chopped fresh chives

1 leek, white part only, cut into matchsticks

8 cherry tomatoes

2 tablespoons chopped fresh parsley

In a small bowl, whisk together all of the vinaigrette ingredients; set aside.

Preheat the oven to 400°F. Using toothpicks, skewer the prawns into closed
circles. Season the fish fillets and prawns with salt and a little of the
vinaigrette. Lightly coat the bottom of a roasting pan with olive oil and add

the fish fillets and prawns. Bake in the preheated oven for about 10 to 12 minutes, or until the fish is just opaque.

Toss the mixed salad greens with the remaining vinaigrette. Mound the greens in the center of each plate and arrange the fish fillets and prawns on top. Decorate the edges of the serving plates with chives and some of the leek. Garnish the salad with cherry tomatoes and sprinkle with the remaining leek and parsley.

Makes 4 servings

Garlic-glazed Fillets of Sole
with Red Pepper Sauce

Filetes de Lenguado Glaseados
con Ajos y Pimientos Dulces

1 teaspoon olive oil

Four 6-ounce sole fillets

Salt and freshly ground pepper to taste

1 cup aïoli (page 178)

Red Pepper Sauce (recipe follows)

2 tablespoons chopped fresh parsley for garnish

Preheat the oven to 350°F. Coat the bottom of a baking dish with the olive oil. Season the sole fillets with salt and pepper and arrange them in one layer in the baking dish. If the fillets are less than 1/4 inch thick, fold them in half end to end.

Bake in the preheated oven until just beginning to turn opaque, 2 to 3 minutes; remove from the oven. (The fish should not be fully cooked at this point.) Spread a thin layer of aïoli on top of the fish. Place the fish under the broiler and broil until the mayonnaise is golden brown, about 3 minutes.

To serve, spoon the red pepper sauce onto 4 plates and arrange the sole fillets on top. Sprinkle with parsley and serve immediately.

Makes 4 servings

RED PEPPER SAUCE

2 tablespoons olive oil

1 onion, minced

2 red bell peppers, roasted, cored, seeded, and chopped (page 185)

1 cup fish stock (page 182) or chicken broth

1 cup heavy (whipping) cream

Salt and freshly ground pepper to taste

In a sauté pan or skillet, heat the olive oil and sauté the onion over medium heat until translucent, about 5 minutes. Add the chopped red peppers and cook for 5 minutes, stirring frequently. Increase the heat to high, add the stock or broth, and bring to a boil. Stir in the cream and reduce the heat to low; continue simmering for 20 minutes. Remove from heat and let cool. Transfer to a blender or food processor and purée. Season with salt and pepper and keep the sauce warm until serving.

Makes about 1½ cups

Asparagus with Almond Sauce

Esparragos Verdes en
Salsa de Almendras

Red pimientos contrast beautifully with green asparagus spears, and the almond sauce is a delicious complement. Almond trees were introduced to Spain by the Moors, and they are basic to many Spanish sauces.

ALMOND SAUCE

1/3 cup blanched almonds, toasted (page 190)

1/2 cup port wine

1 shallot, peeled and chopped

1/4 cup beef broth

1 cup heavy (whipping) cream

Salt and freshly ground pepper to taste

24 asparagus spears

One 7-ounce jar pimientos

To make the almond sauce: Grind the toasted almonds in a blender or food processor. In a saucepan over medium-high heat, place the ground almonds and all the remaining sauce ingredients and bring to a boil. Reduce the heat to low and simmer the sauce for 10 minutes; set aside and keep warm.

Bring a large pot of salted water to a boil. Snap the ends off the asparagus spears and boil uncovered until crisp-tender, about 2 minutes, depending on the size of the spears. Remove from heat and gently run the asparagus under cold water to stop the cooking process and keep the bright green color; drain well.

To serve, spoon the almond sauce onto 4 serving plates. Place 2 bunches of 3 asparagus stalks each in a wedge shape on top of the almond sauce on each plate. Band each bunch decoratively with pimiento strips.

Makes 4 servings

Squab with Dates

Pichon con Datiles

*Dates are an unusual but excellent companion
to squab or game hens.*

24 dates, pitted

1 cup dry white wine

2 large potatoes

6 tablespoons olive oil

Salt and freshly ground pepper to taste

Four 1-pound squabs or Cornish game hens

1 large onion, diced

1 large carrot, peeled and diced

8 garlic cloves

1 bay leaf

1 to 2 tablespoons flour

Soak the dates in the white wine for 12 to 24 hours.

Peel the potatoes and cut them into balls with a melon baller; you should have about 6 balls per person. In a large skillet, heat 3 tablespoons of the olive oil until very hot. Toss in the potatoes, lower heat to medium, and sauté, tossing frequently. When the potatoes begin to brown, lightly sprinkle them with salt and pepper. Continue cooking for about 10 to 15 minutes, or until the potatoes are nicely browned and tender; set aside.

Preheat the oven to 350°F. Heat the remaining 3 tablespoons of olive oil in a deep, heavy casserole or Dutch oven over medium heat and sauté the squabs or game hens until golden brown; transfer to a plate. Pour off most of the fat in the pot and sauté the onion, carrot, and garlic cloves until soft, about 10 minutes. Return the birds to the casserole and add the bay leaf, salt and pepper to taste, and enough water to cover the birds. Raise the heat to high and bring the liquid to a boil. Reduce the heat to low and simmer for 45 minutes.

Remove the birds with a slotted spoon and set them aside on a plate. Strain the liquid through a sieve and return it to the casserole over medium heat. Add the dates, wine, potato balls, and birds; simmer for 5 minutes.

To serve, remove the dates, potato balls, and birds from the casserole with a slotted spoon and set aside. Over high heat, whisk in the flour to thicken the sauce, if necessary. Remove the sauce from heat and season to taste.

Cut the squabs or game hens into quarters, then place them on a platter in their original shape. Surround them with the dates and potato and pour the sauce over.

Makes 4 servings

Ibizan Cheese Tart

Flaó o Tarta de Queso Ibicenco

A cheesecake with an unusual mint and anise flavor.
It can be made the day before a party and kept in the refrigerator.

PASTRY

2 tablespoons butter

1/4 cup sugar

1 egg

1/2 teaspoon anisette liqueur or anise extract

1 teaspoon brandy

1 cup unbleached all-purpose flour

Pinch of salt

1/4 teaspoon aniseed

1/4 teaspoon baking powder

CHEESE FILLING

8 ounces queso fresco or ricotta cheese at room temerature

8 ounces cream cheese at room temperature

2 ounces mild fresh goat cheese

Chopped fresh mint to taste

3 eggs

1 1/3 cups sugar, plus some for sprinkling

To make the pastry: In a large bowl, cream the butter with the sugar then beat in the egg. Stir in the anisette liqueur or anise extract and brandy. Using a wooden spoon, quickly blend in the flour, salt, aniseed, and baking powder. (Do not overmix or the pastry will be tough.) Form the dough into a ball, wrap in plastic wrap, and refrigerate for 3 to 4 hours.

On a lightly floured surface, roll the chilled dough out into a circle about 1/8 inch thick and 1 1/2 inches larger than a 9-inch tart shell or quiche ring. Carefully lay the dough over the pan and trim off any excess dough.

Preheat the oven to 350°F. To make the filling: In a large bowl, beat together the queso fresco or ricotta cheese, cream cheese, goat cheese, and mint until soft and fluffy. In a medium bowl, beat together the eggs and 1 1/3 cups sugar and fold into the cheese and mint mixture, mixing until thoroughly blended. Pour the batter into the prepared crust.

Bake in the preheated oven for about 45 minutes, or until the tart has puffed and trembles just slightly when jiggled. A toothpick inserted in the center will come out almost clean, with just a trace of batter on it. Remove from the oven, let cool to room temperature, then chill for several hours. Remove from the pan and arrange on a platter. Sprinkle the top lightly with sugar.

Makes one 9-inch tart

Hostal de La Gavina

S`Agaró, Spain

Hostal de La Gavina is a luxurious five-star resort overlooking two of the most beautiful beaches of the Costa Brava. The hotel has remained in the Ensesa family since its opening in 1932, and they are responsible for the hotel's extraordinary collection of art and antiques. The Candlelight Room restaurant offers Continental and Catalán cuisine and an internationally known cellar.

MENU

Salmon Rillettes

Marinated Bass and Salmon with Pine Nuts

Beef Tournedos à la Gavina

Lobster Ragoût with Rioja Wine

Pineapple with Catalán Cream

Salmon Rillettes

Rilletes de Salmon Fresco
a la Ciboulette

Serve as a first course, and be sure to remember that cold food needs more seasoning than hot food.

1 pound salmon fillets

1/2 cup (1 stick) butter at room temperature

1 small bunch fresh chives, minced

3 eggs, separated

Juice of 1 lemon

Salt and freshly ground pepper to taste

1 1/2 cups tomato coulis (page 187)

6 tablespoons mayonnaise (page 184)

Mâche or baby lettuces for garnish

Tomato slices for garnish

Place the salmon in a steamer basket over boiling water, cover, and steam for 3 minutes, or until just opaque throughout. Remove from the steamer basket carefully. Let cool and break into pieces; set aside.

In a medium bowl, whip the butter and chives until fluffy. Beat in the egg yolks and lemon juice. Add the salmon and mix by hand until barely incorporated. Add salt and pepper, cover, and refrigerate overnight.

To serve, pool tomato coulis on 6 plates and add a dollop of mayonnaise to each plate. Mold the rillette mixture into olive-shaped quenelles by dipping

2 dessert spoons in hot water and molding the mixture with the spoons. Place 5 quenelles in the center of each plate to form a star shape. Garnish each plate with mâche or baby lettuce leaves and sliced tomatoes.

Makes 6 servings

Marinated Bass and Salmon with Pine Nuts

Duo de Pescados Macerados
con Piñones

Juice of 2 lemons

1/2 cup virgin olive oil

Salt and freshly ground pepper to taste

1 pound bass fillets, skinned

1 pound salmon fillets, skinned

1/2 cup pine nuts for garnish

1 ripe tomato, peeled and diced (page 189), for garnish

2 handfuls mâche or mixed baby lettuces

In a medium bowl, whisk together the lemon juice, olive oil, salt, and pepper.

Place the bass and salmon fillets in separate nonaluminum containers. Pour half of the vinaigrette over each, cover, and marinate the fish for 12 hours in the refrigerator, turning the fillets occasionally.

To serve, thinly slice the marinated fish and arrange on 6 plates. Garnish with pine nuts, diced tomatoes, and mâche or baby lettuces.

Makes 6 first-course servings

Beef Tournedos à la Gavina

T o u r n e d o s   S o u v e n i r   G a v i n a

This is an elegant but easy dish for a special occasion.

4 poached artichoke hearts (recipe follows)

7 ounces fresh duck or goose liver*

Salt and freshly ground pepper to taste

2 tablespoons butter

1/2 cup fresh or thawed frozen corn kernels

1 cup heavy (whipping) cream

Four 6-ounce beef tournedos

Olive oil for sautéing

One 1-ounce can truffles, drained and minced
(reserve the juice for the sauce)

2 tablespoons brandy, preferably Spanish

2 tablespoons port wine

1 cup reduced beef broth

1 tablespoon butter

Clarified butter for sautéing (page 179)

2 carrots, peeled and grated, for garnish

Prepare the artichoke hearts. Slice the liver into 1/4 -inch-thick slices with a sharp knife that has been dipped into boiling water before each slice. Season with salt and pepper. Cover and chill for at least 20 minutes, or until cooking time.

In a sauté pan or skillet over medium-high heat, melt the butter and add the corn kernels and cream. Simmer until the cream thickens enough to coat the back of a spoon. Remove from heat and fill the poached artichoke hearts with the corn mixture; set aside.

Season the beef tournedos with salt and pepper to taste. Film a hot sauté pan or skillet with olive oil, place the beef tournedos in the pan, and cook them for 3 minutes on each side. Remove from the pan, place on a plate, and add the truffles. Cover to keep warm. Reserve the pan with its juices for the sauce.

Pour the brandy and port wine into the pan and cook and stir to scrape up any browned bits on the botttom of the pan. Ignite the liquid with a match and shake the skillet slowly until the flames have subsided. Add the beef broth. Cook over medium heat to reduce the liquid by one half and whisk in the butter; keep warm until serving.

Film the bottom of a sauté pan or skillet with clarified butter and heat until very hot but not burning. Rapidly sauté the duck liver slices one at a time for less than a minute on each side, or until just browned around the edges. Place the duck liver on top of the beef tournedos. Divide the tournedos and stuffed artichoke hearts among 4 plates. Arrange the grated carrot around the artichoke hearts to form flower shapes.

Makes 4 servings

*Duck liver is available at some butcher shops and specialty foods stores. It may be ordered directly from D'Artagnan by calling 800-327-8246 or, in New Jersey, 201-792-0748. Mail orders are available by UPS Next Day Air.

POACHED ARTICHOKE HEARTS

4 large artichokes

1/4 cup fresh lemon juice

5 cups water

1/2 teaspoon salt

Slice the stems off the base of the artichokes. Snap off the outer leaves by pulling them back, then cut off the remaining cone of leaves on top. Brush the cut portions with lemon juice to prevent discoloration. In a stainless steel or enameled pan, simmer the artichoke bottoms in the water, remaining lemon juice, and salt for 30 to 40 minutes, or until they are very tender when pierced with a sharp knife. Let cool, then refrigerate in the cooking liquid until needed.

Shortly before using the artichokes, wash them under cold water and scoop out the choke with a teaspoon. Trim off any tough leaf ends.

Makes 4 artichoke hearts

Note: Artichoke hearts may be prepared in advance and will keep in their cooking liquid for 2 or 3 days in the refrigerator.

Lobster Ragoût with Rioja Wine
Ragoût de Bogabante
al Vino de Rioja

This dish is even better made a day before serving.

4 shallots

3 tablespoons butter

One 1-pound lobster, split in half

1 cup Rioja or other dry red wine

1 cup heavy (whipping) cream

Salt and freshly ground pepper to taste

2 carrots, peeled and finely diced

2 zucchini, finely diced

To a small saucepan of boiling salted water, add 2 of the unpeeled shallots. Reduce the heat to low and simmer until tender, about 25 minutes. Drain, peel, and reserve.

Peel and mince the remaining 2 shallots. In a large sauté pan or skillet over medium heat, melt 2 tablespoons of the butter and add the minced shallots and the split lobster, meat-side down. Sauté and turn the lobster for several minutes, until the lobster shells are bright red.

Add the wine and continue to simmer for 1 minute, then stir in the cream. Season lightly with salt and pepper. Reduce the heat to low and simmer for 20 minutes. Remove the lobster halves and reserve.

In a sauté pan or skillet over low heat, melt the remaining tablespoon of butter and sauté the carrots until almost tender, about 6 minutes. Add the zucchini and poached shallots and sauté until the zucchini are tender, about 3 minutes. Add the vegetables to the lobster sauce. Boil slowly, stirring gently for several minutes, until the sauce has thickened slightly. Correct the seasoning if necessary. Return the lobster halves to the sauce and simmer until they are just heated through. Serve immediately.

Makes 2 servings

Pineapple with Catalán Cream
Piña con Crema Catalana

1 ripe pineapple

1 cup Catalán Cream (page 50)

7 to 8 tablespoons sifted powdered sugar

1 cup heavy (whipping) cream

1/2 teaspoon vanilla extract

Whipped cream for garnish

Cut off the top of the pineapple. Using a sharp knife, cut away the skin, cutting out any eyes. Slice in wedges and cut away the core.

Arrange the pineapple wedges on 6 serving plates and stuff the wedges with Catalán cream.

Place the heavy cream, 6 tablespoons of the powdered sugar, and vanilla extract in a deep bowl and beat until soft peaks form.

To serve, preheat the broiler. Sift a layer of 1 or 2 tablespoons of powdered sugar over the Catalán cream and place the pineapple wedges under the broiler just until the sugar caramelizes, 2 to 4 minutes. Garnish with whipped cream and serve immediately.

Makes 6 servings

Hotel El Castell

La Seu d'Urgell, Spain

Hotel El Castell is the creation of Jaume Tàpies i Travé, who discovered the beauty of this part of the Pyrenees while doing his military service. He built the hotel at the foot of the old Castell fortress, an historic crossroads and center of communications since its days as a Roman fortification. The hotel has exceptional views of the Segre River Valley and the imposing Cadí mountain range and is just six miles from Andorra. Castell's restaurant, which is among the finest and most beautifully appointed in Catalunya, serves Catalán, French, and Spanish dishes featuring game in season and mountain cheeses, and offers an excellent wine list.

M E N U

Cold Crawfish Bisque

Roast Duck with Vegetables

Coho Salmon Stuffed with Mushrooms

Poached Pears in Puff Pastry

Cold Crayfish Bisque

Bisque Fria de Cangrejos de Rio

1 pound crayfish

2 tablespoons butter

2 large onions, diced

3 leeks, white part only, diced

2 tomatoes, diced

1/2 bay leaf

1 fresh thyme sprig

2 to 3 tablespoons Cognac or brandy

3 cups water

1/2 cup heavy (whipping) cream

Salt and freshly ground pepper to taste

Wash the crayfish under cold running water. To devein them, grasp the middle tail fin and give it a sharp twist. It should break off, bringing with it a dark viscera. Remove the tails from 12 of the crayfish and set them aside to chill in the refrigerator.

In a sauté pan or skillet over medium heat, melt the butter and sauté the onions and leeks until translucent, about 5 minutes. Add the tomatoes, bay leaf, and thyme and cook for 5 minutes. Increase the heat to high, add the crayfish, and sauté for 5 more minutes. Add the Cognac or brandy, let it warm, and ignite it with a match. Shake the pan slowly until the flames subside. Add the water, cover the pot, and reduce the heat to low. Simmer for 20 minutes, remove from heat, and let cool.

Purée the vegetables and crayfish in a blender or food processor and strain through a fine sieve. In a medium saucepan, add the purée and cream. Simmer over medium heat for 2 to 3 minutes. Season with salt and pepper. Remove the bisque from heat, let cool, and chill.

To serve, divide the reserved chopped crayfish tails among 4 bowls and pour the chilled bisque over them.

Makes 4 servings

Roast Duck with Vegetables
Caneton de Corral

2 ducks, each about 4 pounds

Salt and freshly ground pepper to taste

4 tablespoons (1/2 stick) butter

3 tablespoons olive oil

2 to 3 tablespoons dry white wine

2 to 3 tablespoons duck pan juices

1 tablespoon chicken broth

2 ounces mushrooms, sliced or quartered (about 3/4 cup)

8 tiny onions

3 carrots, peeled and chopped

3 zucchini, quartered

4 ounces fettuccine

Preheat the oven to 450°F. Pull out the excess fat from the cavity and from around the neck of the ducks. Rinse the ducks well and pat them dry. Prick the skin of the ducks all over, especially on the breast, without piercing the flesh. Cut each duck in half with kitchen shears or a large knife. Chop the wings off at the elbows and remove the wishbone. Season inside and out with salt and pepper.

In a small saucepan over low heat, melt 2 tablespoons of the butter and combine with 1 tablespoon of the olive oil. Brush the duck with the butter-oil mixture and transfer to a roasting pan, breast-side up. Bake in the preheated oven for 20 minutes. Remove from the oven leaving the oven on, and let rest for 5 minutes. Carve by removing the leg-thigh sections first and then removing the wings.

Return the thigh-leg sections to the oven and continue roasting until they reach 180°F when a thermometer is inserted into the inner thigh or the juices run rosy when the thigh is pierced with a knife, about 25 minutes. Set aside and cover to keep warm, reserving the pan juices. Slice the breast meat into strips and cover to keep warm.

Break the duck carcasses into pieces. In a stockpot over high heat, cook the carcass and white wine until the liquid is reduced by one half, about 5 minutes. Add the drippings and chicken broth and boil down until syrupy. Skim off any fat and strain the sauce through a fine sieve.

In a small saucepan over medium heat, heat the remaining 2 tablespoons of the olive oil and sauté the onions until they are translucent, about 5 minutes. Reduce the heat to low and add just enough water to cover the onions. Cover the pan and simmer until the onions are quite tender, about 25 minutes.

In a pot of boiling salted water, cook the carrots for 10 minutes. Add the zucchini and cook for another 10 minutes. Drain the vegetables and set aside.

In a medium skillet over high heat, melt the remaining 2 tablespoons of butter and sauté the mushrooms for 10 minutes; set aside.

In a pot of boiling salted water, cook the fettuccine until al dente, about 7 minutes for dried pasta and 2 to 3 minutes for fresh; drain.

Arrange the duck, pasta, carrots, zucchini, onions, and mushrooms on a serving platter. Spoon the sauce over and serve at once.

Makes 4 servings

Coho Salmon Stuffed with Mushrooms
Trucha Salmonada Rellena de Ceps

Four 8-ounce coho salmon

Salt and freshly ground pepper to taste

1 teaspoon butter

1 cup (3 ounces) wild or cultivated white mushrooms, sliced

1 garlic clove, minced

1½ ounces goose liver pâté*

1 teaspoon minced fresh parsley

1 teaspoon snipped fresh chives

LEMON CREAM SAUCE

½ cup dry white wine

2 shallots, minced

1 cup heavy (whipping) cream

Juice of ½ lemon

½ cup (1 stick) plus 2 tablespoons cold butter, cut into small pieces

Salt and freshly ground pepper to taste

Preheat the oven to 400°F. Fillet the salmon, removing all bones and skin, and season with salt and pepper.

In a sauté pan or skillet over high heat, melt the butter. When the butter foams, toss in the mushrooms. Sauté for several minutes, then add the garlic and sauté for 1 minute. Remove from heat. Stir in the pâté, parsley, and chives, and mix well. Add salt and pepper to taste.

On a large work surface, lay out 4 of the fish fillets. Evenly divide the mushroom mixture among the fillets, spreading it over each one. Cover each fillet with one of the remaining 4 fillets. Cut baking parchment or aluminum foil into 3 rectangles and brush the edges with olive oil. Arrange 1 double fillet in the center of one half of each parchment or foil piece. Fold the remaining half of the parchment or foil over the fish and seal the packet by folding in the edges. Place the 4 packets in a baking dish and bake in the preheated oven for 8 to 10 minutes.

Meanwhile, make the lemon-cream sauce: In a small saucepan over high heat, boil the white wine and shallots until the liquid is reduced by one third. Add the cream, lemon juice, salt, and pepper. Remove the saucepan from heat and immediately whisk in 2 pieces of the butter. As the butter melts, whisk in another piece. Set the saucepan over very low heat and, whisking constantly, continue adding more butter as each previous piece has almost melted into the sauce. The sauce should become a thick ivory-colored cream, the consistency of a light hollandaise. Serve immediately, or set over barely tepid water to keep warm.

To serve, pool the lemon sauce onto 4 plates. Open the packets, remove the fish fillets, and arrange them on top of the lemon sauce; serve immediately.

Makes 4 servings

* Goose liver is available at some butcher stores or specialty foods shops, or you may order it directly from D'Artagnan by calling 800-327-8246 or, in New Jersey, 201-792-0748. Mail orders are available by UPS Next Day Air.

Poached Pears in Puff Pastry

H o j a l d r e   d e   P e r a   W i l l i a m s

3/4 cup sugar

2 cups water

2 ripe Bosc or Bartlett pears, peeled, halved lengthwise, and cored

1 sheet frozen puff pastry

1 cup pastry cream (page 185)

1/2 cup whipped cream

Sugar for sprinkling

1/4 cup Williams pear liqueur or other pear liqueur

1 cup crème anglaise (page 180)

In a medium saucepan, bring the sugar and water to a simmer over medium heat, stirring until the sugar just dissolves; remove from heat. Peel, halve, and core the pears. Place the pear halves in the saucepan with the sugar syrup immediately in order to prevent discoloration. Poach the pears over low heat until tender when pierced with a sharp knife, about 10 minutes. (Keep just below a simmer, as simmering will burst the fruit.)

Remove the pan from heat and let the pears cool in the syrup. Remove the pears with a slotted spoon and cut each pear half lengthwise into 3 wedges; set aside.

Preheat the oven to 425°F for about 20 minutes while the puff pastry dough thaws at room temperature. On a lightly floured surface, roll out the dough out into a 6- by 12-inch rectangle; prick all over with a fork.

Cover a baking sheet with parchment paper or grease it with butter and place the puff pastry on top. Bake in the preheated oven for 25 minutes, or until puffed and golden brown. Let the pastry cool, then cut it with a serrated knife into four 2- by 4-inch rectangles. Cut off the tops to make 4 lids. Scoop out the insides of the bottom rectangles.

To serve, preheat the broiler. In a small bowl, combine the pastry cream and whipped cream. Fill the 4 puff pastry bottoms with the cream mixture and cover with pastry lids. Arrange half a poached pear cut into very thin slices on top of each lid. Sprinkle the pears with sugar and place under the broiler just until the sugar begins to caramelize, about 2 minutes. Spoon 1 tablespoon pear liqueur or brandy over each pastry. Pool 1/4 cup warm crème anglaise onto each of 4 plates and arrange the pear pastries on top.

Makes 4 servings

Hotel La Bobadilla

L o j a - G r a n a d a ,   S p a i n

La Bobadilla is a magnificent hotel complex created by Rudolf Karl Staab to resemble an Andalusian village, both rustic and sophisticated. Everything at this resort is simply the best. La Bobadilla is located near the legendary city of Granada on a magnificent 1,750-acre estate. Sheep, pigs, and several types of birds are bred on the hotel farm, and no chemicals are used in the kitchen gardens or orchards. The award-winning La Finca restaurant is one of the best in Spain and offers international haute cuisine.

M E N U

Potato Salad with Salmon and Champagne Vinaigrette

Tricolored Pepper Bisque

Sole with Pistachio Sauce

Chicken with Sesame Seeds and Leek Sauce

Mango Mousse with Mango Sherbet

Potato Salad with Salmon
and Champagne Vinaigrette

Ensalada de Patatas con Medallones de
Salmona la Vinagreta de Cava

Serve this salad as a first course for dinner
or as a light luncheon.

CHAMPAGNE VINAIGRETTE

6 tablespoons peanut oil

6 tablespoons virgin olive oil

1/4 cup champagne or sherry wine vinegar

Salt and freshly ground pepper to taste

6 new potatoes, peeled and halved

2 shallots

4 handfuls mixed baby lettuces

4 cups fish stock (page 182) or chicken broth

Four 3-ounce salmon fillets, or two 6-ounce salmon fillets cut in half

In a small bowl, whisk all the vinaigrette ingredients together; set aside.

Place the potatoes in a pot of cold salted water to cover. Bring to a boil and cook until the potatoes are tender when pierced with a knife, about 20 minutes. Drain the water and cut the potatoes, while still warm, into 1/4-inch-thick slices. In a medium bowl, combine the potato slices with the shallots and one third of the vinaigrette.

Toss the salad greens with one third of the vinaigrette until all the leaves are lightly coated.

In a medium saucepan, heat the stock or broth until just below simmering. Poach the salmon fillets in the liquid until just opaque throughout, about 3 minutes, then remove the fillets with a slotted spatula. Remove any skin and sprinkle with the remaining vinaigrette.

Arrange the lettuce on 4 plates, top with the potatoes and salmon, and serve.

Makes 4 servings

Tricolored Pepper Bisque

Crema de Pimientos de Tres Colores

*The three contrasting colors of the peppers make this soup
beautiful as well as delicious.*

3 red bell peppers

3 green bell peppers

3 yellow bell peppers

6 tablespoons olive oil

6 shallots, minced

2 1/4 cups heavy (whipping) cream

3 3/4 cups veal stock (page 190) or beef broth

Salt and freshly ground pepper to taste

Cut the bell peppers into quarters, discard the cores and seeds, and slice into thin strips, being careful to keep the different-colored peppers separate. In a saucepan over medium heat, heat 2 tablespoons of the olive oil and sauté one third of the shallots until translucent, about 2 minutes. Add only the red pepper slices and cook over medium-high heat for 5 minutes, stirring frequently. Add 3/4 cup of the cream and 1 1/4 cups of the veal stock or beef broth. Bring the mixture to a boil, then reduce heat to low and simmer for 40 minutes. Repeat with the green and then the yellow bell peppers. Do not mix the different-colored peppers.

In a blender or a food processor, separately purée each of the 3 different-colored pepper mixtures until smooth. In 3 separate saucepans, cook the puréed soup over low heat for 5 minutes, or until slightly thickened. Add salt and pepper.

To serve, ladle 3 large spoonfuls of each color of pepper purée into each of 6 shallow soup bowls, being careful to keep the colors separate.

Makes 6 servings

Sole with Pistachio Sauce

P e z   S a n   P e d r o   a   l a   S a l s a
d e   P i s t a c h o s   V e r d e s

1 cup heavy (whipping) cream

1 cup fish stock (page 182) or chicken broth

5 ounces unsalted pistachio nuts, shelled

1/2 cup dry white wine

3 tablespoons butter, cut into pieces

1 1/2 to 2 pounds sole fillets

Salt and freshly ground pepper to taste

2 tablespoons olive oil

4 handfuls of baby lettuces, or 8 ounces fettuccine cooked until al dente

2 tablespoons unsweetened whipped cream for garnish

In a medium saucepan over high heat, rapidly boil down the cream and stock or broth until the mixture thickens enough to lightly coat the back of a spoon, about 5 minutes. Remove from heat, let cool, and transfer to a blender or food processor. Add the pistachio nuts and purée until smooth. Return the purée to the saucepan and stir in the wine. Whisk in a piece of the butter and, as the butter melts, whisk in another piece until all of the butter has been added. The sauce should thicken and attain the consistency of a light hollandaise. Cover and keep the sauce warm over barely tepid water while preparing the fish.

Season the fish fillets with salt and pepper. In a sauté pan or skillet over medium-high heat, heat the olive oil and sauté the fish until lightly browned on both sides ; remove from the pan and cover to keep warm.

Arrange the baby lettuces or noodles on 4 plates and place the fish fillets on top. Spoon the pistachio sauce over the fish, garnish with a dollop of unsweetened whipped cream, and serve immediately.

Makes 4 servings

Chicken with Sesame Seeds and Leek Sauce

Pechuga de Capon de Nuestra Granja
en Mantel de Sesamo
a la Salsa de Puerros

*The crispy sesame seed-coated chicken breasts are topped
with leek sauce for a delicious combination of flavors.*

LEEK SAUCE

5 leeks, white part only

2 tablespoons olive oil

1 medium potato, peeled and cut into small dice

1 cup chicken broth

1/2 cup dry white wine

1 cup heavy (whipping) cream

Salt and freshly ground pepper to taste

1/4 teaspoon ground nutmeg

4 boneless chicken or capon breasts

Salt and freshly ground pepper to taste

1/4 cup flour

1 egg, beaten

1/2 cup raw sesame seeds

2 tablespoons walnut oil

2 tablespoons olive oil

To make the leek sauce: Split the leeks in half lengthwise, wash well, and dry. Cut 8 halves into thin strips about 2 inches long and cut 1 of the remaining halves into julienne (reserve the last half for another use.) In a large, heavy saucepan over medium heat, heat the olive oil and sauté the leek strips until translucent, about 5 minutes. Add the potato, chicken broth, wine, and cream. Simmer until the potato and leeks are cooked and the liquid has reduced slightly, about 20 minutes. Remove from heat, strain the sauce through a sieve, and return it to the saucepan. Stir in the julienned leek and season with salt, pepper, and nutmeg. Cook over medium heat for 5 minutes, or until slightly thickened. Set aside and keep warm.

Season the chicken or capon breasts with salt and pepper. Dip them in the flour, then in the beaten egg, and finally dredge them in the sesame seeds. In a large, heavy sauté pan or skillet, heat the walnut and olive oils over medium-high heat and sauté the breasts until just opaque throughout, about 4 minutes on each side.

To serve, place the breasts on individual plates or on a large platter. Spoon the leek sauce over and serve immediately.

Makes 4 servings

Mango Mousse with Mango Sherbet
Mousse de Mango con Su Sorbete

MANGO SHERBET

1/4 cup sugar

1/4 cup water

1/2 cup dry white wine

1 ripe mango, peeled and diced (1 cup)

3 tablespoons mango nectar (optional)

2 tablespoons maraschino liqueur or kirsch

MANGO MOUSSE

1/2 cup dry white wine

1/3 cup sugar

1 ripe mango, peeled and diced (1 cup)

1 envelope plain gelatin

1/4 cup cold water

2 1/4 cups heavy (whipping) cream

1 tablespoon mango nectar (optional)

To make the sherbet: In a saucepan over medium heat, bring the water and sugar to a simmer, but do not boil. Remove from heat as soon as the sugar has completely dissolved; let cool to room temperature.

In a saucepan over medium-high heat, cook the wine and diced mango for 5 minutes. Remove from heat and let cool. Transfer to a blender or food processor and purée. Press the mango purée through a fine sieve into a medium bowl, using the back of a spoon. Stir in the sugar syrup, mango nectar, and maraschino liqueur. Freeze in an ice cream maker according to the manufacturer's instructions.

To make the mousse: In a saucepan over medium heat, bring the wine and sugar to a simmer, but do not boil. Remove from the heat as soon as the sugar has completely dissolved. Add the diced mango pieces and cook for 5 minutes. Remove from heat and let cool. Purée in a blender or food processor and set aside.

In a small bowl, soak the gelatin in the water for 5 minutes. In a small saucepan, combine the gelatin and puréed mango. Simmer until the gelatin dissolves, but do not boil. Remove from heat and allow the mixture to cool to room temperature.

In a deep bowl, whip the cream until soft peaks form. Gently fold the whipped cream into the cooled mango purée. Add the optional mango nectar and blend until smooth; chill in the refrigerator.

Several hours before serving, place 4 individual serving bowls in the freezer to chill. Spoon the mousse and sherbet into the chilled bowls and serve.

Makes 4 servings

Hotel Santa Marta

Lloret de Mar, Spain

Hotel Santa Marta offers luxurious accommodations in a peaceful setting of great beauty on the Costa Brava. The hotel's fifteen acres of parks and gardens sweep down to the seashore. The excellent restaurant is noted for Catalán specialties and French cuisine.

MENU

Salmon Rolls with Crab

Seafood Crêpes Florentine

Veal Scallops Flavored with Tarragon

Glazed Asparagus with Smoked Fish

Walnuts Flambé with Grand Marnier

Salmon Rolls with Crab

Rollitos de Salmon Fresco
con Cangrejos

1 tablespoon olive oil

1/2 small onion, minced

12 ounces shredded fresh or thawed frozen crab meat

1 tablespoon brandy, preferably Spanish

1 tablespoon fresh tomato purée

1 1/3 pounds center-cut salmon fillets

Salt and freshly ground pepper to taste

1 cup tartar sauce (page 189)

Truffle Vinaigrette (recipe follows)

In a sauté pan or skillet over medium heat, heat the oil and sauté the onion and crab meat for 2 minutes. Pour in the brandy, let it warm, ignite it with a match, and shake the skillet slowly until the flames subside. Stir in the tomato purée and remove from heat; let cool.

Slice the salmon fillets very thinly crosswise. Season with salt and pepper. Lay each slice of salmon flat and spoon some of the crab mixture on the bottom third of each fillet. Roll into a fat sausage shape and place seam side down in an oiled baking dish. Refrigerate until chilled. To serve, divide the rolls among 6 plates, top each with a spoonful of tartar sauce, and season with a dash of truffle vinaigrette.

Makes 6 servings

TRUFFLE VINAIGRETTE

3 tablespoons sherry wine vinegar

3 tablespoons balsamic vinegar

1/4 cup walnut oil

1/2 cup olive oil

1/4 teaspoon minced garlic

1 teaspoon minced canned black truffle

2 tablespoons truffle juice (from the can or jar in
which the truffle was packed)

Salt and freshly ground pepper to taste

In small bowl, combine all of the ingredients. Cover and refrigerate until using.

Makes 1 1/4 cups

Seafood Crêpes Florentine
Crêpes de Mariscos Florentina

2 tablespoons olive oil

1 pound medium shrimp, shelled

12 ounces monkfish or other firm white-fleshed fillets,
skinned and chopped

Salt to taste

1 tablespoon brandy, preferably Spanish

2 tablespoons tomato sauce (page 188)

3/4 teaspoon minced fresh tarragon, or 1/4 teaspoon dried tarragon

1 tablespoon flour

12 crêpes (page 180)

1 1/2 cups chopped cooked spinach

Hollandaise sauce (page 183)

In a sauté pan or skillet over high heat, heat the olive oil and sauté the shrimp, and chopped fish fillets until the shrimp turns pink 3 to 4 minutes. Season with salt. Reduce the heat to medium and pour in the brandy. Let it warm, ignite it with a match, and shake the skillet slowly until the flames subside. Stir in the tomato sauce, tarragon, and flour and simmer, stirring, for 2 or 3 minutes. Remove from heat and let cool.

Place a spoonful of the seafood mixture on the lower third of each crêpe and roll into a cylinder. Place the crêpes and spinach on plates seam-side down and pour the hollandaise sauce over.

Makes 6 servings

Veal Scallops Flavored with Tarragon

E s c a l o p i t a s   d e   T e r n e r a
P e r f u m a d a s   a l   E s t r a g o n

3 eggs

2 cups unbleached all-purpose flour

Twelve 3-ounce veal scallops, pounded 3/8 inch thick

1 teaspoon salt

1/4 cup olive oil

1/2 onion, diced

2 pounds wild or cultivated white mushrooms, sliced

11/2 teaspoons minced fresh tarragon, or 1/2 teaspoon dried tarragon

1/4 cup brandy, preferably Spanish

2 cups Spanish sauce (page 186)

In a shallow bowl, beat the eggs together. Place the flour in another shallow bowl. Season the veal scallops with salt and dip them in the egg mixture, then in the flour. Shake off any excess flour.

In a sauté pan or skillet over high heat, heat a little of the olive oil until very hot but not smoking. Place several veal scallops in the pan in one layer and sauté for 1 minute on each side. Remove them to a platter and cover to keep warm. Add more olive oil to the pan as needed and sauté the remaining veal scallops, cover and set aside.

In the same skillet over medium heat, sauté the onion until translucent, about 5 minutes. Increase the heat to high and add the mushrooms and tarragon. Pour in the brandy, let it heat, ignite it with a match, and shake the frying pan until the flames have subsided. Stir in the Spanish sauce.

To serve, arrange the veal scallops on a platter and pour some of the sauce over. Pass the remaining sauce.

Makes 6 servings

Glazed Asparagus with Smoked Fish

E s p a r r a g o s   G l a s e a d o s   c o n   A h u m a d o s

36 to 48 fresh asparagus spears

12 ounces smoked fish fillets

Hollandaise sauce (page 183)

Preheat the broiler. Snap the tough ends off the asparagus spears. Boil the asparagus in salted water to cover for about 2 minutes, or until the spears can be pierced with a fork but are still crunchy. Drain and immediately plunge the asparagus into cold water to stop the cooking process and keep the bright green color.

Dry the asparagus on paper towels, place them on an ovenproof platter, and spoon the hollandaise sauce over. Place under the broiler until the sauce is a light golden brown. Divide the asparagus and smoked fish among 6 serving plates and serve at once.

Makes 6 servings

Walnuts Flambé with Grand Marnier

Nueces Flambeadas al Grand Marnier

7 tablespoons butter

8 ounces (2 cups) walnuts

1/2 cup Grand Marnier

8 ounces bittersweet or semisweet chocolate, cut into pieces

1/4 cup heavy (whipping) cream

Vanilla ice cream

In a sauté pan or skillet over medium heat, melt the butter and add the walnuts; sauté until slightly browned. Pour in the Grand Marnier, let it warm, ignite it with a match, and shake the skillet slowly until the flames subside; set aside.

Place the chocolate and cream in the top of a double boiler over simmering water and melt the chocolate, stirring constantly. Add the nuts, Grand Marnier, and butter and cook for several minutes.

To serve, place scoops of vanilla ice cream into 6 dessert bowls and spoon the warm sauce over. Serve immediately.

Makes 6 servings

Iberia Restaurant

Portola Valley, California

Iberia Restaurant, nestled in the wooded hills of Portola Valley, serves dishes representative of most regions of Spain. The restaurant is a reflection of the personal taste and style of chef-owners Jose Luis and Jessica Relinque. Born in Seville and raised in Barcelona, Jose Luis moved to California at age twenty and has since been active in the restaurant business in the San Francisco Bay Area. Jessica has many jobs at the restaurant, but her favorite pastime is growing produce for the restaurant in the couples' extensive kitchen garden. The Relinques take frequent trips to Spain and have recently begun to develop culinary itineraries for customers and friends planning visits to Spain.

M E N U

Cream of Almond Soup

Scallops with Brandy

Beef Tenderloin Asturias

Figs Stuffed with Pistachios and Chocolate

Cream of Almond Soup

C r e m a   d e   A l m e n d r a s

This refreshing white gazpacho keeps well in the refrigerator for several days. It may also be drunk as a nutritious beverage.

12 slices French bread, crusts removed

Milk for soaking

8 ounces (2 cups) blanched almonds

1/2 cup olive oil

1½ tablespoons sherry wine vinegar

8 garlic cloves

5½ cups water

Salt to taste

20 to 36 peeled grapes for garnish (optional)

Croutons for garnish (page 181)

Soak the bread slices in milk and squeeze dry. In a blender or food processor, purée all the ingredients except the salt and garnishes. Season with salt and chill in the refrigerator until serving. Ladle the soup into bowls and garnish with 5 or 6 peeled grapes per person and fried bread cubes.

Makes 4 to 6 servings

Scallops with Brandy
Vieras al Brandy

3 tablespoons olive oil

1 shallot, minced

2 garlic cloves, minced

3 tablespoons minced fresh parsley

3 Roma (plum) tomatoes, peeled, seeded, and puréed (page 189)

1/3 cup Amontillado (medium) sherry

1/4 cup brandy, preferably Spanish

1 cup cubed smoked bacon

1 small dried hot red pepper, crushed

16 sea scallops

Salt to taste

In a sauté pan or skillet over medium-high heat, heat the olive oil. Add the garlic and sauté for 2 minutes. Add the shallot and sauté until translucent, about 3 minutes. Add the parsley and tomatoes and cook until the mixture begins to thicken. Add the sherry and continue cooking until the mixture thickens again; set aside.

In a sauté pan or skillet over medium heat, fry the bacon and red pepper until most of the bacon fat is rendered. Increase the heat to high, add the scallops, and stir until golden, about 2 minutes. Drain off the excess bacon fat. Add the tomato sauce and cook over high heat until the mixture is bubbling. Add salt. Pour in the brandy, let it warm, ignite it with a match, and shake the skillet until the flames have subsided. Serve at once.

Makes 4 servings

Beef Tenderloin Asturias

S o l o m i l l o   A s t u r i a s

Four 6-ounce beef filet steaks, trimmed of fat

Salt and freshly ground pepper to taste

1/4 cup olive oil

1 small onion, minced

1 tablespoon paprika

4 ounces Cabrales cheese* or other creamy blue-veined cheese

1/4 cup dry white wine

1/2 cup reduced beef broth

2 tablespoons chopped fresh parsley

Season the steaks with salt and pepper. In a heavy skillet over medium-high heat, heat the olive oil. Sear the steaks on both sides and cook almost to the point of desired doneness. Remove and keep warm.

Add the onion to the skillet over medium heat, and sauté until translucent, about 5 minutes. If it begins to stick, add a tablespoonful of water to the pan. Add the paprika and cook for 1 more minute. Add the white wine and brown stock and bring to a boil; cook until the sauce is reduced by half. Add the cheese and cook until it just melts, stirring constantly. Blend in any pan juices from the steaks and add salt and pepper. Arrange the steaks on 4 serving plates and spoon the sauce over. Sprinkle with parsley and serve at once.

Makes 4 servings

* Cabrales cheese is available from La Española in Lomita, Calfornia. Telephone 310-539-0455, or fax 310-539-5989.

Figs Stuffed with Pistachios and Chocolate

Higos Rellenos de Pistachios y Chocolate

This dessert deserves applause!

1 cup water

1 cup red wine

1/2 cup Grand Marnier

28 dried figs

1/4 cup sugar

4 ounces bittersweet chocolate, chopped

1 cup (4 ounces) walnuts, chopped

1 cup (4 ounces) pistachios, chopped

Whipped cream for garnish

In a large saucepan over high heat, bring the water, red wine, Grand Marnier, and sugar to a boil. Add the figs, reduce heat to low, and simmer for 30 minutes. Remove the figs with a slotted spoon and set aside. Increase heat to high and cook the sauce to reduce it until it is as thick as honey.

In a medium bowl, mix the chocolate, walnuts, and pistachios together. Make a hole in each poached fig with your finger and stuff the fig with this mixture.

Arrange the figs on serving plates and spoon some of the warm sauce over. Garnish with dollops of whipped cream.

Makes 4 to 6 servings

Landa Palace

Burgos, Spain

Landa Palace includes a fourteenth-century Castillian tower and is on the historic road to Santiago de Compostela. The hotel has been a lifetime labor of love for owners Señor and Señora Landa, both artists. They have furnished Landa Palace with collections of antiques and installed a music pavillion once in the main plaza of Burgos in the hotel's main courtyard. The restaurant, Salón Real, is the region's finest, serving local specialties and inventive dishes in a stunning setting of stone walls, Gothic arches, and huge hand-wrought chandeliers.

MENU

Marinated Partridge

Clams and Beans

Stewed Potatoes with Chorizo

Custard-filled Pastries

Marinated Partridge

Perdiz Escabechada

The method of preserving food by stewing it in a marinade of oil, vinegar, and herbs was brought to Spain by the Moors. At Landa Palace, this dish is prepared during the winter hunting season and stored for serving in the summer.

2 cups dry white wine

Eight 1-pound partridges or Cornish game hens

2 cups olive oil

3 onions, julienned

6 garlic cloves, chopped

2 cups dry white wine

6 cups sherry wine vinegar or red wine vinegar

2 bay leaves

1 fresh thyme sprig

1 teaspoon ground black pepper

Gherkins, olives, and tomatoes for garnish

In a medium saucepan over high heat, cook the white wine until it is reduced by half; set aside.

Truss the partridges or game hens with cotton string so they keep their shape. Heat 3 tablespoons of the olive oil in a large, heavy pot into which the birds will fit snugly in one layer. Brown the birds in batches, turning them until they are golden brown on all sides and adding more olive oil as necessary. Transfer to a platter.

In the same pot over medium heat, heat 3 tablespoons of the olive oil and sauté the onions until translucent, about 5 minutes. Add the garlic and sauté for 1 minute. Push the vegetables to the sides of the pot and add the birds, reduced white wine, vinegar, bay leaves, thyme, pepper, and remaining olive oil and bring to a boil. Reduce the heat to low, cover, and simmer for about 1 hour, adding water as necessary to keep the birds completely covered. Remove the pot from heat and let cool to room temperature. Remove the birds with a slotted spoon, discard the trussing string, and place the birds in a large glass or crockery bowl.

Spoon the fat from the liquid in the pot, correct the seasoning, and strain through a sieve. Pour the liquid over the hens to completely cover them. Cover the bowl and refrigerate for 2 or 3 days. The stock will jell around the birds.

To serve, cut the birds in half with kitchen shears and remove the backbones. Place the jelled liquid over very low heat until just liquified, but not warm. Arrange the birds on a platter with a little of the sauce. Garnish with gherkins, olives, and tomatoes. Serve, passing the remaining sauce.

Makes 8 servings

Clams and Beans

A l u b i a s   c o n   A l m e j a s

*The restaurant at Landa Palace serves this savory dish
in a beautiful copper casserole.*

6 ounces (2/3 cup) dried white beans, soaked overnight in salted water

1 carrot, peeled and chopped

1 onion, quartered and cut crosswise into 1/4-inch-thick slices

1 leek (white part only), quartered lengthwise and
cut into 1/4-inch-thick slices

4 ounces clams in the shell

2 tablespoons olive oil

3 garlic cloves, minced

3 tablespoons flour

Salt and freshly ground pepper to taste

1/4 cup minced fresh parsley

Discard the soaking water from the beans and place the beans, carrot, onion, and leek in a large pot with fresh water to cover. Bring the water to a boil over high heat; reduce the heat to low and simmer until the beans are tender, about 1 1/2 hours. Add more water as needed to keep the beans covered. Drain the water and return the beans and vegetables to the pot; set aside.

While the beans are cooking, place the clams in a bowl with salted water to cover and let sit for 1 hour.

In a large sauté pan or skillet, heat the olive oil over medium-high heat. Sauté the garlic until golden and stir in the clams and flour. Remove the pan from heat. Add water to almost cover the clams. Return the pan to medium-high heat and boil until the clam shells open, about 4 minutes. Season with salt, pepper, and chopped parsley.

Combine the stewed clams with the beans and return the pot to high heat. Let boil for 1 minute. Transfer to a serving dish and serve immediately.

Makes 8 servings

Stewed Potatoes with Sausage

P a t a t a s   G u i s a d a s   c o n   C h o r i z o

*This slow-simmering potato and sausage stew makes
a simple one-pot meal.*

3 tablespoons olive oil

1 onion, chopped

1/2 green bell pepper, cored, seeded, and chopped

1/2 red bell pepper, cored, seeded, and chopped

4 chorizo sausages or other pork sausages, sliced

6 potatoes, peeled and coarsely cubed

2 garlic cloves

2 tablespoons minced fresh parsley

2 tablespoons white wine or potato cooking liquid

Salt and freshly ground pepper to taste

In a large skillet over medium heat, heat the olive oil and sauté the onion until translucent, about 5 minutes. Add the bell peppers and cook for 5 minutes, stirring frequently. Add the sausage slices and potatoes and continue frying for 5 minutes. Add just enough water to barely reach the top of the potatoes and bring to a rapid boil. Reduce heat to low, cover, and simmer gently for 35 minutes. Most of the liquid will be absorbed and a thick sauce will form from the pieces of potato that fall apart.

In a mortar, crush the garlic cloves and chopped parsley together with a pestle. Moisten the mixture with a little white wine or potato liquid and mix into the bell peppers, onions, potatoes, and sausages. Cover and cook for the last 10 minutes. Season with salt and pepper, and serve steaming hot.

Makes 4 to 6 servings

Custard-filled Pastries

Bartolillos

Fried pastries are traditional in Spain where in the past few homes had ovens but olive oil was plentiful. These delicious empanada-shaped pastries are filled with custard and dusted with sugar.

1³/4 cups sifted unbleached all-purpose flour

1/2 cup (1 stick) butter or lard

1 teaspoon salt

1/3 cup dry sherry

1¹/2 cups pastry cream (page 185)

Olive oil for deep-frying

1 lemon slice

1 orange slice

Sifted powdered sugar for dusting

In a medium bowl, stir together the flour and salt and cut in the butter or lard until crumbly. Add the sherry and mix the dough quickly into a ball. Turn out onto a lightly floured board and knead very briefly, adding only enough additional flour to make a dough that doesn't stick to your hands. Form into a ball, cover with plastic wrap, and refrigerate for at least 2 hours.

Roll out the chilled dough on a lightly floured board to a thickness of 1/8 inch and cut into eight 4-inch squares. Place a spoonful of pastry cream in the center of each square, then fold the square over to cover the cream. Cut the pastry into a semicircular shape like an empanada. Crimp the edges with the tines of a fork.

In a large, heavy pot or deep-fryer, pour olive oil to a depth of 2 inches. Add the lemon and orange slices and heat to 375°F, or until almost smoking. Carefully drop the pastries into the hot oil in small batches, and cook, turning once, until deep golden, about 1 minute on each side. Remove each batch with a slotted spoon and drain on paper towels to absorb the excess oil. Transfer to a serving dish and dust with sugar before serving.

Makes 8 servings

Marbella Club Hotel

Marbella, Spain

The Marbella Club Hotel offers accommodations at the highest possible level on Spain's Costa del Sol. The lushly landscaped property consists of Andalusian-style bungalows with private swimming pools and gardens ending at the beach. The Marbella Club Restaurant is a celebrity rendezvous that moves from indoors to an outdoor terrace according to the season.

MENU

Duck Liver a l'Orange

Rice with Crayfish

Souffléd Raspberry Crêpes

Duck Liver à l'Orange
Higado de Pato a la Naranja

ORANGE SAUCE

1 tablespoon butter

1 small shallot, minced

1 cup port wine

Juice of 2 oranges

3 tablespoons beef broth

Salt and freshly ground pepper to taste

7 ounces fresh duck liver*

Salt and freshly ground pepper to taste

Clarified butter (page 179)

Orange zest for garnish

To make the orange sauce: In a sauté pan or skillet over medium heat, melt the butter and sauté the shallot until translucent, about 2 minutes. Add the port, orange juice, and beef broth. Cook over medium heat to reduce the liquid by half. Season with salt and pepper. Set aside and keep warm.

Slice the duck liver into 1/4-inch-thick slices with a sharp knife that has been dipped in boiling water before each slice. Season with salt and pepper. Cover the slices and chill for at least 20 minutes, or until cooking time. (The liver is chilled so that a minimum of fat will exude during the cooking.) Film the bottom of a sauté pan or skillet with the clarified butter and heat to very hot but not burning. Rapidly sauté the duck liver slices 1 at a time for less than 1 minute on each side, or until just browned around the edges, adding more clarified butter as necessary.

To serve, spoon some orange sauce into the middle of each of 2 plates. Place the duck liver slices on top of the sauce, spoon some sauce over, and sprinkle with orange zest.

Makes 2 servings

* Duck liver is available at some butcher shops and specialty foods stores. It may be ordered directly from D'Artagnan by calling 800-327-8246 or, in New Jersey, 201-792-0748. Mail orders are available UPS Next Day Air.

Rice with Crayfish

Arroz con Cigalitas

*Crayfish (or "crawfish") are freshwater shellfish that look
like tiny lobsters. There are two types available in North America,
one from Louisiana and one from the West Coast.*

1 pound crayfish or prawns

2 cups hot fish stock (page 182) or chicken broth

1 cup olive oil

1 small onion, diced

1 garlic clove, minced

1 small tomato, diced

1/4 teaspoon saffron threads

1/2 teaspoon salt

1 cup Arborio rice

Preheat the oven to 250°F. Wash the crayfish in running water. To eviscerate them, grasp the middle of the 3 tail flaps and give it a sharp pull and twist. The vein will pull out with the fin. Reserve 4 crayfish or prawns for garnish.

In a medium saucepan, bring the fish stock to a simmer. Cover and keep warm over low heat.

In a paella pan or large skillet, heat the olive oil over medium-high heat. Sauté the onion until translucent, about 5 minutes. Add the garlic and tomato and sauté for a few minutes on low heat. Meanwhile, crush the saffron threads with the salt in a mortar. Add a teaspoonful of broth to make a smooth paste and stir the paste into the vegetable mixture. Add the rice and sauté until it is opaque. Stir in the hot broth and remove from heat.

Transfer the pan to the preheated oven and bake until the rice is almost tender, about 30 minutes. Remove the pan from the oven and cover with aluminum foil. Let stand for 10 minutes and serve garnished with the 4 reserved crayfish.

Makes 4 servings

Souf, léd Raspberry Crêpes

Crêpes Soufflé de Frambuesas

This soufflé within a crêpe makes a dramatic dessert.

CREPES

½ cup unbleached all-purpose flour

1 tablespoon sugar

2 tablespoons butter, melted

2 eggs

½ cup milk

⅛ teaspoon salt

3 tablespoons clarified butter (page XX)

4 eggs, separated

4 tablespoons pastry cream (page XX)

½ cup raspberry liqueur (framboise)

⅓ cup sugar

1 cup raspberries

To make the crêpes: Using a whisk or blender, combine the flour, sugar, melted butter, eggs, milk, and salt until perfectly smooth. Cover and chill for 1 hour.

Heat a 7-inch crêpe pan or skillet until drops of water dance on it, then brush it lightly with clarified butter. Pour approximately ¼ cup of the batter into the center of the pan and tilt the pan to spread the batter evenly. Cook the crêpe until the bottom is lightly browned, about 30 seconds, then flip it over and cook for another 15 to 20 seconds. Remove from the pan and set crêpe aside to cool on a cake rack. Repeat until all the batter is used, adding clarified butter as necessary.

Preheat the oven to 375°F. In a medium bowl, whisk together the egg yolks, pastry cream, and raspberry liqueur. In a large bowl, beat the egg whites until soft peaks form, then continue beating at high speed and sprinkle in the sugar; continue beating until the egg whites form stiff peaks. Gently fold into the egg yolk and raspberry mixture.

Fold the 4 crêpes in half, best side out, and arrange them in back to back pairs in a buttered baking dish. Unfold the crêpes 1 at a time, add one fourth of the raspberries to each crêpe, scoop one fourth of the soufflé mixture into each, and lay the top crêpe half back in place. At once, set on the middle rack of the preheated oven and bake until the soufflés have puffed the crêpes open, about 12 minutes. Serve immediately.

Makes 4 servings

Mas de Torrent

Girona, Spain

The Figueras family has restored and converted an eighteenth-century Catalán manor house into a small hotel and excellent restaurant in the heart of the Costa Brava. The Arati restaurant offers a carefully created menu of Catalán, Basque, and French cuisine and a well-provided cellar. In the evenings and afternoons when the weather is pleasant, Arati adds to its charm by opening its terrace.

MENU

Vegetable Soup with Shrimp and Basil

Veal Scallops with Artichoke Sauce

Fish Fillets with Aïoli

Lemon Caramel Cream

Vegetable Soup with Shrimp and Basil

Minestrone de Gambas con Albahaca

1 bunch basil, stemmed

1/4 cup chicken broth

4 tablespoons olive oil

1 onion, minced

2 garlic cloves, minced

1/2 cup finely diced peeled carrots

1/2 cup finely diced celery

1/2 cup finely diced green beans

1 large tomato, peeled, seeded, and diced (page 189)

1/2 cup finely diced zucchini

6 cups fish stock (page 182) or chicken broth

2 dozen large shrimp, shelled and deveined

Salt and freshly ground pepper to taste

Place the basil and chicken broth in a blender and purée; set aside.

In a skillet over medium heat, heat 2 tablespoons of the olive oil and sauté the onion until translucent, about 5 minutes. Add the garlic and sauté for 1 minute.

Add the carrots and celery and sauté until soft. Add the green beans, zucchini, and tomato and sauté for 3 minutes.

In a large soup pot over high heat, add the stock or broth and sautéed vegetables. Bring to a boil, then reduce the heat to low. Add 2 tablespoons of the basil purée and simmer for 30 minutes.

In a skillet or frying pan over high heat, heat the remaining 2 tablespoons of olive oil and sauté the garlic and shrimp for 2 or 3 minutes, or until the shrimp turn pink. Stir in 2 tablespoons of the basil purée (reserve the remaining purée for another use). Add salt and pepper.

Divide the shrimp evenly among 6 to 8 shallow soup bowls and pour the soup over.

Makes 6 to 8 servings

Veal Scallops with Artichoke Sauce

Medallón de Ternera Blanca
con Velouté de Alcachofas

ARTICHOKE SAUCE

8 artichokes

4 cups chicken broth

1 cup heavy (whipping) cream

Salt and freshly ground pepper to taste

2 tablespoons cold butter, cut into 1/2-inch dice

2 tablespoons olive oil

2 carrots, chopped

4 shallots or 2 small yellow onions, peeled and chopped

3 parsley sprigs, 1/2 bay leaf, and 2 thyme sprigs tied in a cheesecloth bag

2 cups dry white wine

Four 3-ounce veal scallops, pounded until thin

Flour for dredging

1/2 tablespoon olive oil

11/2 tablespoons butter

To make the artichoke sauce: Cut the artichokes into hearts as described on page 93. Poach 4 of the artichoke hearts in simmering salted water to cover until tender, about 30 to 40 minutes; set aside. In a saucepan over medium-high heat, bring the chicken broth and cream to a boil and cook to reduce by half. Reduce the heat to low and continue simmering until the sauce thickens enough to coat the back of a spoon. Season with salt and pepper.

In a blender or food processor, purée the 4 poached artichoke hearts. Mix this purée into the sauce and strain the sauce through a sieve. Return to the saucepan to low heat and whisk in the butter pieces a few at a time. Place the sauce over barely warm water until serving.

In a large skillet over medium-low heat, heat the olive oil and sauté the 4 raw artichoke hearts until they are just beginning to color, about 3 to 4 minutes. Add the carrots, shallots or onions, herbs, and white wine. Reduce heat to low and simmer for about 10 minutes, or until the artichokes are tender when pierced with a sharp knife.

Dredge the veal scallops in the flour until lightly covered. In a skillet over high heat, heat the olive oil and butter. When the butter foam has almost subsided, add the veal and sauté for 2 minutes, then turn and sauté for 2 more minutes.

To serve, spoon the sauce onto 4 dinner plates and arrange the veal and sliced artichoke hearts on top.

Makes 4 servings

Fish Fillets with Aïoli

F i l e t e   d e   D o r a d a   c o n   S a l s a
d e   A ï o l i   S u a v e

6 gilt-head bream, sea bass, or salmon fillets, boned and skinned

Salt and freshly ground pepper to taste

1½ cups fish mousse (recipe follows)

2 small zucchini

2 Roma (plum) tomatoes

2 cups aïoli (page 178)

4 garlic cloves

Preheat the oven to 350°F. Pat the fish dry and go over it with your fingers to remove any remaining bones. Season lightly with salt and pepper. Using a spatula, top the fish fillets with the mousse and place them in a buttered baking dish. Cover and refrigerate.

Cut the zucchini and the tomatoes into thin crosswise slices. Overlap the zucchini and tomato slices on top of the fish mousse to resemble fish scales.

Place the garlic cloves in a small saucepan of simering water and poach for 10 minutes; drain. Add the poached garlic cloves to the aïoli and purée. Add enough water to make a sauce.

Lightly oil a baking dish and add the decorated fish fillets. Bake in the preheated oven for 5 to 7 minutes, or until the fish is just opaque throughout.

To serve, divide the aïoli among 6 serving plates, top with the fish fillets, and serve immediately.

Makes 6 servings

FISH MOUSSE

1 pound sole fillets, chopped

1 large egg

1/2 cup chilled heavy (whipping) cream, or more as needed

1 teaspoon salt

Freshly ground white pepper to taste

Pinch of ground nutmeg

Fine soft bread crumbs as needed (optional)

Place the fish in a blender or food processor along with the egg, cream, salt, pepper, and nutmeg. Purée or process with six 1-second spurts, then for several seconds continuously. The mousse should be perfectly smooth. Scrape down the sides and process a few seconds more, if necessary. The mousse should hold its shape in a spoon. If the mousse is too thin, add some fine bread crumbs, and if it is too stiff, add more cream.

Makes about 1 1/2 cups

Note: Fish mousse may be made several hours in advance and kept covered in the refrigerator in a bowl of ice.

Lemon Caramel Cream
Crema de Limón Caramelizada

A delicious lemon-flavored custard with caramel topping.

1 cup plus 1 tablespoon sugar

1 cup strained fresh lemon juice

7 egg yolks

4 cups heavy (whipping) cream

Preheat the oven to 300°F. In a small, heavy skillet over medium-high heat, melt 6 tablespoons of the sugar until it turns a light golden color. Immediately remove the pan from heat, pour the caramel into a 2-quart mold, and tilt to coat the bottom of the dish.

In a small saucepan over high heat, boil the lemon juice until it has reduced by one fourth. Pour the cream into a medium, heavy saucepan and scald over medium-high heat. Remove from heat and set aside.

In a medium bowl, beat the egg yolks and remaining 3/4 cup plus 1 tablespoon sugar together for 10 minutes, or until pale and thick. Pour the hot cream into the egg mixture in a slow, steady stream, whisking continually. Whisk in the lemon juice.

Pour the custard into the prepared mold and place in a baking dish. Pour water into the dish to halfway up the sides of the mold. Cover with aluminum foil and bake in the preheated oven for about 50 minutes, or until the custard is set around the edges and quivers slightly in the center.

Let cool to room temperature and refrigerate for several hours to overnight before serving.

Makes 6 to 8 servings

Restaurant Juan Arzak

San Sebastián, Spain

Restaurant Juan Arzak is one of Spain's great restaurants. With three Michelin stars, it is a required stop in the Basque region for anyone interested in either creative or traditional food. Chef-owner Juan Mari Arzak pioneered nueva cocina vasca, or "new Basque cuisine," which changed fine dining in Spain as nouvelle cuisine changed fine dining in France. Arzak continues to influence cooking all over Spain.

MENU

Fish Baked in Salt with Fried Vegetables

Grilled Squid with Ink Sauce

Arzak Lobster Salad

Pheasant in Pastry

Cheese Ice Cream with Fruit Purée

Fish Baked in Salt with Fried Vegetables
Rodaballo con Verduras Fritas

*Coarse sea salt forms a case for turbot or flounder, sealing
in all the delicious juices. Measure the thickest part of the fish and
allow 15 minutes for every 3/4 inch, or about 20 minutes for a fish
weighing 1 1/2 pounds. Cracking and removing the salt case at
tableside makes a dramatic presentation.*

VINAIGRETTE

2 tomatoes, peeled, seeded, and diced (page 189)

1 1/4 cups olive oil

1/4 cup sherry wine vinegar

Salt and white pepper to taste

1 tablespoon minced fresh chives

3 leeks, white part only

8 ounces spinach, stemmed

1 large turnip, peeled

2 beets, peeled

Four 8-ounce turbot or flounder fish fillets, with skin

Salt and freshly ground pepper to taste

To make the vinaigrette: In a small bowl, combine all the vinaigrette
ingredients. Chill in the refrigerator for 24 hours before using.

Preheat the oven to 375°F. Rinse the leeks well and cut them into very fine
julienne. Remove the stems from the spinach. Using a mandoline, slice the
turnip and beets into thin slices.

In a skillet over medium-high heat, add olive oil to a depth of about 1/4 inch and heat until very hot but not smoking; a faint vapor will rise from the surface. Lower the heat to medium-high. Fry the leeks, spinach, turnip, and beets each in turn until they are tender but still crunchy. Remove the vegetables with a slotted spoon and drain on paper towels.

Season the fillets with salt and pepper. Butter a baking dish and cover the bottom with a layer of coarse rock salt. Place the fish fillets, skin-side up, in one layer on top of the salt, and completely cover them with more of the salt. Bake in the preheated oven and remove when done. Crack the salt crust and very carefully peel it off; the skin of the fish will probably adhere to the salt.

Arrange the fish fillets on 4 serving plates and spoon the vinaigrette on top. Cover with the fried vegetables and serve immediately.

Makes 4 servings

Grilled Squid with Ink Sauce

Calamar a la Parrilla con Vinagreta Caliente

Squid is enormously popular in Spain, and squid served with its ink is a Basque specialty.

3 1/2 pounds squid

1 1/2 cups olive oil

3 shallots

3 tablespoons minced fresh parsley

2 onions, cut into julienne

4 small green bell peppers, cored, seeded, and cut into julienne

VINAIGRETTE

3 tablespoons red wine vinegar

3 tablespoons white wine vinegar with herbs

1 garlic clove, crushed

3 tablespoons brandy, preferably Spanish

SQUID INK SAUCE

1/3 cup olive oil

1 1/2 cups chopped onions

2 green bell peppers, cored, seeded, and diced

2 garlic cloves, minced

2 tomatoes, chopped

1 rosemary sprig

1/2 cup red wine

Reserved squid ink sacs

8 rosemary sprigs for garnish

To clean the squid, first pull away each body from the head and tentacles. Reserve the tiny silver ink sacs for the squid ink sauce. Cut the tentacles from the head and discard the head along with the attached intestine. Pull the flat spine from the body and discard. Strip away the thin outer membrane. Wash the bodies well, then turn them inside out and wash again. Using scissors, cut the squid bodies down the long side and open flat. Using a sharp knife, cut into diamond shapes.

In a nonaluminum bowl, whisk together 1 cup of the olive oil, shallots, and parsley. Add the tentacles and squid pieces, cover, and marinate them in the refrigerator for about 12 hours.

To make the vinaigrette: In a small bowl, whisk together all the vinaigrette ingredients; set aside.

In a medium bowl, marinate the onions and green peppers in the remaining 1/2 cup of olive oil for 15 minutes. In a sauté pan or skillet over medium heat, heat 3 tablespoons of the olive oil and sauté until the onions and green peppers are soft, about 10 to 15 minutes; set aside.

Prepare a fire in a charcoal grill. While the coals are heating, make the ink sauce: In a large sauté pan or skillet over medium heat, heat the olive oil and add the onions, green peppers, garlic, tomatoes, and rosemary. Reduce heat to low and simmer until the vegetables are tender, about 20 minutes. Add the red wine and cook slowly for 10 more minutes. Break the ink sacs with the back of a spoon and stir the ink into the sauce. Strain the sauce through a fine sieve; set aside and keep warm.

Remove the squid from the marinade and skewer the squid pieces and tentacles. When the coals are hot, cook the squid until lightly golden, then turn, baste with a little of the vinaigrette, and cook until the other side is golden.

To serve, place the onion and pepper base in the center of each of 4 plates. Remove the squid from the skewers and arrange on top. Spoon some squid ink sauce over and decorate with a rosemary sprig on either side.

Makes 4 servings

Arzak Lobster Salad

Ensalada de Bogavante de Arzak

VINAIGRETTE

6 tablespoons walnut oil

2 tablespoons sherry wine vinegar

Salt to taste

One 1 1/2 -pound lobster

1/4 cup olive oil

3 tablespoons sherry wine vinegar or red wine vinegar

2 handfuls mixed greens such as baby lettuce,
escarole, and watercress, torn into pieces

Pink Mayonnaise (recipe follows)

2 tablespoon finely juilienned leeks

2 tablespoons minced fresh chives

1 tablespoon minced fresh chervil

In a small bowl, whisk all the vinaigrette ingredients together.

In a large pot, boil enough salted water to cover the lobster. Plunge the lobster into the water, let the water return to a boil, and boil for 5 minutes. Remove the lobster from the pot and place in a pan of ice water to stop the cooking process. Cut the lobster in half with a large knife and separate the tail from the body. Remove the shells from the tail and claws, leaving the meat whole. Cut through the underside of the tail, remove the tail meat in large pieces, and slice. Place the lobster meat on a plate. In a small bowl, combine the olive oil and 1 tablespoon of the vinegar. Pour over the lobster and set aside.

To serve, toss the mixed greens with the vinaigrette. Place the greens in a mound in the center of 2 serving plates. Arrange the warm lobster meat on top. Garnish each plate with a dollop of pink mayonnaise and sprinkle with the leeks and chives. Decorate with the lobster claws and sprinkle with chervil.

Makes 2 servings

PINK MAYONNAISE

1/2 cup mayonnaise

1 tablespoon Ketchup

2 tablespoons orange juice

1 tablespoon heavy (whipping) cream

In a small bowl, stir together all the ingredients; set aside.

Makes 3/4 cups

Pheasant in Pastry
Pan de Faisan

This is a dish for special occasions. Pheasant is a lean game bird with the largest breast of all the game birds. Two Cornish game hens may be substituted if pheasant is unavailable.

PASTRY

6 tablespoons cold butter

3 to 3 1/2 cups unbleached all-purpose flour

1 egg

3/4 cup water

1 pheasant (about 2 pounds)

Salt to taste

1/2 fennel bulb

1 fresh or canned truffle, sliced

3 apples, peeled, cored, and chopped

Minced salt pork or bacon slices for basting

To prepare the pastry: In a large bowl, cut the butter into the flour with a pastry cutter or 2 knives until crumbly. Add the egg and water and mix with a fork. Form into a ball and knead briefly on a lightly floured surface until the dough is smooth. Chill for at least 30 minutes.

Preheat the oven to 475°F. Rinse the pheasant and pat dry. Season the pheasant with salt. Trim the bottom off the fennel bulb, peel off the wilted outer layer, and cut the bulb into julienne. Make cuts in the pheasant breast and insert the truffle and fennel slices into them. Stuff the pheasant cavity with the apples. Smear the pheasant with the salt pork or cover with bacon slices.

On a lightly floured surface, roll the pastry out into a 1/8-inch-thick circle large enough to cover the pheasant completely. Lay the pastry over the pheasant, fit it tightly, and press the edges of the pastry together on the bottom. Cut several vent holes in the pastry and plunge a meat thermometer through one of these vents into the inner thigh of the pheasant. Bake in the preheated oven for about 1 hour, or until the meat thermometer reaches 180° to 185°F.

Remove the pheasant from the oven and transfer to a platter. To serve, cut the pheasant in half and serve immediately.

Makes 2 servings

Cheese Ice Cream with Fruit Purée

Helado de Queso Fresco Sobre
Crema de Patxaranes

At Restaurant Juan Arzak, this dessert is made with patxaranes,
a kind of berry that grows only in the Basque country. Red currants,
raspberries, or strawberries are good substitutes.

1 pound (4 cups) queso fresco,* ricotta cheese, or
dry cottage cheese at room temperature

1 cup sugar

1 cup milk

3/4 cup heavy (whipping) cream

FRUIT PURÉE

1/4 cup sugar

1 cup water

4 cups red currants, raspberries, or strawberries

Heavy cream and mint leaves for garnish

In a large bowl, beat the cheese until soft and creamy. Beat in the cream, milk, and sugar until all the ingredients are very well blended. Strain through a fine sieve. Freeze in an ice cream machine according to the manufacturer's instructions.

Meanwhile, make the fruit purée: In a small saucepan, combine the sugar and water. Bring to a simmer, stirring constantly, until the sugar dissolves. Cover and simmer for 5 minutes. Remove from heat, uncover, and let cool.

Place the berries and the sugar syrup in a blender and purée. Strain through a fine sieve.

To serve, spoon the fruit purée onto 4 dessert plates. Draw designs with some heavy cream in the fruit purée. Place balls of cheese ice cream on top and decorate them with mint leaves.

Makes 4 servings

* Queso fresco is a mild white cheese available in Latino markets.

Sol y Luna

San Francisco, California

Sol y Luna is a center for fine food and entertainment in an avant-garde setting in San Francisco's Financial District. The restaurant offers live music four nights a week, including flamenco dancers backed by the house band, Grupo Sol y Luna. The critically acclaimed food emphasizes tapas, paella, and seafood dishes.

MENU

Spanish Omelette

Garlic Soup

Paella with Seafood

Caramel Custard

Spanish Omelette
Tortilla Española

*This classic dish, a round, flat omelette that contains
potatoes and onion, should be golden brown on the outside and moist on the
inside. It may be served hot, warm, or cold. Cut the tortilla
into squares for tapas, or enjoy it for lunch or as a picnic dish.*

1/4 cup olive oil

4 potatoes, peeled and diced

1/2 onion, chopped

Salt to taste

6 eggs

In a 9-inch skillet, heat the olive oil until very hot but not smoking. In a
medium bowl, mix together the potatoes, onion, and salt and add to the pan.
Reduce the heat slightly and cook for about 15 minutes, turning with a
spatula 2 or 3 times. When the potatoes are quite tender and golden, place a
plate over the frying pan and drain the olive oil into a small bowl. Set the
potatoes aside in a strainer.

In a medium bowl, beat the eggs together and season with salt to taste. Stir
the potatoes and onion into the eggs and mix well.

In the same skillet over high heat, heat 2 tablespoons of the drained olive oil
until very hot. Pour in the egg, potato, and onion mixture and spread the
potatoes evenly. With your right hand, hold a wooden spoon in the middle of
the fying pan; move the pan clockwise with the left hand and the spoon
counterclockwise for about 20 seconds. This prevents the omelette from
burning in the center.

Reduce heat to low and cook the omelette for about 5 minutes, shaking the pan occasionally to make sure the bottom isn't sticking. When the top of the egg mixture is no longer liquid, place a plate over the pan and drain off the olive oil into a small bowl. Turn the omelette out onto a plate. Return the olive oil to the frying pan. Slide the omelette back in to cook on the reverse side for 2 or 3 minutes. Remove the omelette by sliding it out onto a serving plate.

Makes 4 to 6 first-course servings

Garlic Soup

S o p a   d e   A j o

Simple, nourishing sopa de ajo is served in the winter, and it is often served free as a restorative on New Year's Day in Spain.

6 to 8 garlic cloves, minced

2½ teaspoons salt

6 slices French bread, crusts removed

5 cups boiling water

½ teaspoon freshly ground pepper

6 tablespoons olive oil

1 teaspoon paprika

4 eggs, beaten

¼ teaspoon ground cumin

Preheat the oven to 350°F. In a small bowl, combine half of the garlic with ½ teaspoon of the salt. Sprinkle the bread slices with the garlic-salt mixture. Bake in the oven for 10 minutes and set aside.

In a large soup pot over high heat, bring the water, remaining 2 teaspoons salt, and pepper to a boil.

In a skillet over medium heat, heat the olive oil and sauté the remaining garlic until light golden, about 2 minutes. Stir in the paprika for 5 seconds, being careful not to burn it. Immediately remove from heat and add the garlic and paprika to the boiling water. Add the bread slices and boil for 30 seconds. Remove the pot from heat. Add the eggs to the hot broth, stirring constantly to form threads. Stir in the cumin and serve.

Makes 4 servings

Paella with Seafood

P a e l l a M a r i n e r a

Paella, a rice dish that may be studded with shellfish, meat, sausages, and vegetables, is one of the great Spanish contributions to gastronomy. It originated in the area around Valencia, where rice is grown extensively. Be sure to eat the golden brown, crunchy rice scraped from the bottom of the pan; this is the socarrat and is considered to be the best part of the paella. Paella marinera, an all-seafood paella, is a great party dish.

1 dozen mussels (see Note)

1 dozen clams (see Note)

1/4 cup olive oil

3 garlic cloves, minced

1 onion, diced

2 tomatoes, peeled, seeded, and chopped (page 189)

1 pound large shrimp, shelled and deveined

8 ounces squid, cleaned and cut into rings

8 ounces scallops, rinsed and patted dry

2 cups Arborio rice

4 cups hot chicken broth

1/2 teaspoon saffron threads

1/2 teaspoon paprika

2 teaspoons salt

8 to 10 blanched asparagus spears for garnish

1/2 cup cooked peas for garnish

1 red bell pepper, roasted, cored, seeded, and thinly
sliced (page 185), for garnish

Lemon wedges and minced Italian parsley for garnish

Place the mussels and clams in a pot with water to cover and bring to a boil. Reduce heat to low and simmer until the shells open, about 5 minutes. Remove from heat and let cool slightly. Discard any shells that do not open. Remove the mussels and clams with a slotted spoon, transfer to a plate, and set aside. Reserve the cooking liquid for later use.

Heat the olive oil in a paella pan or 14-inch skillet over medium heat. Sauté the garlic and onion until translucent, about 5 minutes. Add the tomatoes and cook until the mixture is quite dry. Add the shrimp, squid, and scallops and sauté until they are just opaque, about 3 minutes. Raise the heat to high and stir in the rice until it is slightly opaque. Add the hot broth. In a mortar, crush the saffron, paprika, and salt together. Add a little of the liquid from the paella to make a smooth paste, then stir it into the paella. Bring to a boil, reduce heat to low, and cook the paella uncovered for 15 minutes without stirring. Add the clams and mussels and continue cooking until the liquid is absorbed, the clams and mussels have opened, and the rice is al dente. Remove from heat.

Decorate the paella with asparagus, peas, red pepper, and lemon wedges. Sprinkle with some Italian parsley and serve immediately.

Makes 6 servings

Note: The mussel and clam shells should be tightly closed. To store them, place in a bowl with water to cover and 1 teaspoon salt. Just before cooking, scrub the shells and pull off the beards from the mussels. (Do not debeard the mussels until just before cooking or they will die and spoil.)

Caramel Custard
Flan

*Flan, a delicious custard with a caramel topping, is Spain's
most popular dessert.*

3/4 cup sugar

2 cups milk

4 eggs

1 vanilla bean, split lengthwise, or 1 1/2 teaspoons vanilla extract

Preheat the oven to 350°F. In a small, heavy saucepan, place 1/2 cup of the sugar and cook over medium heat until it turns golden. Remove from heat and pour the caramel into a single 6-cup mold or six 6-ounce custard cups, tilting to coat the bottom molds.

In a small saucepan over medium heat, bring the milk and the vanilla bean, if using, slowly to the boiling point. Remove from heat and set aside. Add the vanilla extract now, if using.

In a medium bowl, beat the eggs together, then gradually beat in 2 tablespoons of sugar. Remove the vanilla bean from the hot milk, if using. Whisk the hot milk into the eggs and transfer to the caramel-coated molds. Place in a baking dish and add hot water halfway up the sides of the mold(s). Bake in the preheated oven for about 40 minutes, or until a knife inserted into the center of the custard comes out clean. Let cool, chill in the refrigerator, and unmold onto a serving plate or plates.

Makes 6 servings

Basics

Aïoli

Used since Roman times, this classic Catalán sauce corresponds to the garlic mayonnaise of Provence. It is eaten with grilled or roast meat, fish, and vegetables, and with bread as a tapa in many bars. Prepare the day before using to allow the flavors to develop.

2 tablespoons minced garlic

1 egg at room temperature

1½ cups olive oil

1 tablespoon fresh lemon juice

½ teaspoon salt

In a blender or food processor, blend the garlic with the egg. With the motor running, add the olive oil in a very slow stream until the aïoli is thick. Add the lemon juice and salt and blend again.

Makes about 1½ cups

Brown Sauce

¼ cup olive oil

1 tablespoon minced onion

1 tablespoon minced peeled carrot

2 tablespoons flour

1¾ cups reduced beef broth or more as needed

1 cup dry white wine

1 tablespoon tomato purée

1 bay leaf

2 parsley sprigs

1/4 teaspoon dried thyme

1/2 cup dry sherry

In a large, heavy skillet over medium heat, heat the olive oil and add the onion and carrot. Cook until the onion is golden, stirring occasionally, about 5 minutes. Sprinkle with the flour and stir until browned. Slowly add the beef broth, stirring constantly until boiling. Add all the remaining ingredients and cook over low heat for 2 hours, stirring occasionally and skimming off any fat that rises to the surface.

Remove from heat and let cool. Purée in a blender or food processor. The sauce should be thick enough to coat the back of a spoon; if it is too thin, cook it a little longer. Add more beef broth if the sauce becomes too thick. Season to taste.

Makes about 2 1/2 cups

Clarified Butter

1/2 cup (1 stick) butter, cut into pieces

In a heavy saucepan, melt the butter over low heat until it crackles and bubbles. Remove the pan from the heat and use a spoon to carefully skim off the foam that has risen to the surface. Pour the clear yellow liquid into a container, leaving the milky residue at the bottom; cover. The butter will keep for months in the refrigerator or freezer.

Makes about 6 tablespoons

Crème Anglaise

2 egg yolks

1/4 cup sugar

2/3 cup hot milk

1 teaspoon vanilla extract

Whisk the egg yolks in a medium saucepan, adding the sugar by spoonfuls. Continue whisking for 2 to 3 minutes until the mixture is pale and thick. By dribbles, add the hot milk, stirring constantly.

Set the saucepan over medium-low heat, stirring constantly with a wooden spoon. The sauce should gradually come near the simmering point. Do not let it simmer or the yolks will scramble. The sauce is done when it coats the back of the spoon. Stir in the vanilla and let cool.

Makes about 1 cup

Note : This sauce can be prepared several days in advance and kept refrigerated.

Crêpes

4 eggs

1 1/3 cups milk

1 cup unbleached all-purpose flour

1/4 teaspoon salt

6 tablespoons butter, melted

In a medium bowl, whisk together the eggs, milk, flour, salt, and 3 tablespoons of the butter until perfectly smooth. Cover and let the batter rest for 1 hour in the refrigerator before cooking.

Heat a 7-inch crêpe pan or skillet until drops of water dance on it, then brush lightly with a little of the remaining butter. Pour 1/4 cup of the batter into the center of the pan and tilt it to spread the batter evenly. Cook the crêpe until the bottom is lightly browned, about 30 seconds, then turn and cook for another 15 to 20 seconds. Remove from the pan and place on a cake rack to cool. Repeat until all the batter is used, brushing the pan with more melted butter when necessary.

Makes 12 crêpes

Croûtons

4 slices French bread, crusts removed

Olive oil for brushing

Brush the bread evenly with olive oil on both sides. Cut the bread into 1-inch cubes and toss in a hot skillet filmed with olive oil until golden brown.

Makes about 1 1/2 cups

Fish Stock

3 pounds fish heads, bones, and trimmings

1 celery stalk, chopped

1 onion, chopped

1 carrot, peeled and chopped

1 bay leaf

4 parsley sprigs

Salt and freshly ground pepper to taste

Wash the fish parts well. In a large pot, place the fish, celery, onion, carrot, bay leaf, parsley, and water to cover by 1 inch. Bring to a boil and skim off the foam as it rises to the surface. Cover and simmer for 30 minutes.

Immediately remove from heat and strain through a sieve. Season with salt and pepper.

Makes about 8 cups

Hollandaise Sauce

6 egg yolks

2 tablespoons fresh lemon juice

1½ cups (3 sticks) unsalted butter, melted

2 tablespoons heavy (whipping) cream

Salt to taste

In the top of the double boiler over barely simmering water, whisk the egg yolks and lemon juice together until smooth. Gradually whisk in the melted butter in a slow, steady stream; the yolks will emulsify into a thick sauce. Whisk in the cream and salt. Serve immediately or keep warm over barely tepid water.

Makes about 2 cups

Lemon or Orange Zest

Using a zester, vegetable peeler, or sharp paring knife, make thin strips of the colored part of the lemon or orange zest; don't include the white pith underneath, which is apt to be bitter.

Mayonnaise

*There is some evidence that this famous sauce was first used in
Port Mahón on the Spanish island of Menorca. The Duke of Richelieu,
chief of the French invading forces, supposedly discovered it there in 1756.
He later popularized the sauce in Paris, calling it sauce mahonnaise.
Mayonnaise is a basic preparation that is thoroughly at home in
Spain, even in the simplest of kitchens.*

2 egg yolks

1 cup olive oil

2 tablespoons fresh lemon juice

1 teaspoon Dijon mustard

1/2 teaspoon salt

Place the egg yolks in a blender or food processor and process for 30
seconds. With the machine running, add the olive oil very slowly, pouring it
in a thin stream. When the mayonnaise is thick, add the lemon juice,
mustard, and salt and process again.

Makes about 1 1/2 cups

Pastry Cream

3 egg yolks

1/4 cup sugar

2 tablespoons cornstarch

1 cup plus 2 tablespoons milk

1/2 vanilla bean, split, or 1/2 teaspoon vanilla extract

In a medium bowl, whisk together the egg yolks and 1 tablespoon of the sugar until the yolks are thick and pale. Sift in the flour and mix well. In a small saucepan, combine the milk, the remaining sugar, and vanilla bean, if using; bring to a boil. Remove from heat and whisk a small amount into the egg mixture. Transfer the mixture back into the saucepan and cook over low heat until it thickens enough to coat the back of a spoon. Remove from heat and remove the vanilla bean, if using. Add the vanilla extract now, if using.

Makes about 1 1/2 cups

Note: Pastry cream may be made ahead and refrigerated for several days.

Roasting and Peeling Peppers

Char the peppers under a broiler or over an open flame until blackened all over. Using tongs, transfer the peppers to a paper bag, close it, and let the peppers cool for 15 to 20 minutes. Remove from the bag, peel off the skin with a small sharp knife, and core, and seed the peppers.

Spanish Sauce

3 tablespoons olive oil

1/2 cup minced onion

3 tablespoons flour

3 cups beef or chicken broth

1 cup tomato sauce (page 188)

2 garlic cloves, minced

1/2 teaspoon dried thyme

1 small celery stalk

1/2 cup chopped peeled carrot

1 bay leaf

2 parsley sprigs

1 teaspoon sugar

1 teaspoon water

3 tablespoons sherry wine vinegar

1/4 teaspoon anchovy paste

Salt and freshly ground pepper to taste

In a medium saucepan over medium heat, heat 2 tablespoons of the olive oil and sauté the onion until translucent, about 5 minutes. Add the remaining 1 tablespoon olive oil, stir in the flour and cook, stirring, until lightly browned. Add the broth, tomato sauce, garlic, thyme, celery, carrot, bay leaf, and parsley.

In a small, heavy saucepan over high heat, cook the sugar with the water until golden; remove from heat and immediately add the vinegar. Mix in the anchovy paste and add this mixture to the sauce. Add salt and pepper and bring the sauce to a boil. Reduce the heat to low and simmer for 30 minutes.

Makes 2 cups

Tomato Coulis

2 pounds (8 to 10) ripe tomatoes

Salt and Tabasco sauce to taste

Drop the tomatoes into a pot of boiling water for 1 to 2 minutes, remove with a slotted spoon, and place in a bowl of ice water. Cut out a small cone around the stem ends and slip off the tomato skins. To seed the tomatoes, cut each in half and gently squeeze each half over a bowl, or a sieve if you want to save the juice. The seeds will drop out. Pick out any remaining seeds with your fingers or a spoon. In a blender or food processor, pureé the tomatoes, salt, and Tabasco.

Makes about 2 cups

Tomato Sauce

3 tablespoons olive oil

1 onion, chopped

1 garlic clove, minced

4 pounds tomatoes, peeled, seeded, and chopped (page 189)

1 teaspoon salt

1/4 teaspoon ground cumin

1/4 teaspoon ground pepper

1 bay leaf

1 tablespoon chopped fresh parsley

1/2 cup water

In a saucepan over medium heat, heat the olive oil and sauté the onion until translucent, about 5 minutes. Add the garlic and sauté for 1 minute. Increase heat to high, add the tomatoes, and cook for several minutes. Add all of the remaining ingredients. Reduce heat to low and simmer for 45 minutes. Remove from heat and purée in a blender or food processor.

Makes about 3 cups

Tartar Sauce

1 1/2 cups good-quality mayonnaise

2 to 3 capers, minced

1 small sour dill pickle, minced

1 hard-cooked egg

3 tablespoons minced fresh herbs such as parsley, tarragon, and chives

Salt and freshly ground pepper to taste

Fresh lemon juice to taste

In a medium bowl, mix together the mayonnaise, capers, and pickle. Halve the egg, sieve the yolk, and add to the bowl. Chop the egg white. Add the chopped white and herbs and blend together. Season with salt, pepper, and lemon juice. Cover and refrigerate until using.

Makes about 2 cups

Peeling and Seeding Tomatoes

Remove the cores from the tomatoes and score the opposite ends with a paring knife in an "X" pattern. Drop them into a pot of rapidly boiling water for 3 to 4 seconds, or until the skin by the "X" peels away slightly. Drain and run cold water over the tomatoes; the skin should slip off easily. To seed, cut the tomatoes in half crosswise and gently squeeze out the seeds.

Toasting Almonds

Place the almonds on a baking sheet in a preheated 350°F oven for 8 to 10 minutes, or until very lightly browned. Whole roasted nuts may be stored in an airtight container in the refrigerator or freezer.

Veal Stock

2 pounds veal bones

2 tablespoons oil

1 onion, chopped

1 carrot, peeled and chopped

1 celery stalk, chopped

½ cup dry white wine

Salt and freshly ground pepper to taste

Preheat the oven to 400°F. In a roasting pan, toss the bones with the oil and vegetables. Brown for 30 to 40 minutes, turning occasionally. Transfer the bones and vegetables to a large saucepan or kettle.

Pour the fat out of the roasting pan. Pour the wine into the pan and place over medium heat, stirring to remove any browned bits on the bottom of the pan. Pour this liquid into the saucepan with the bones and vegetables. Add water to cover the ingredients by 1 inch. Bring to a boil and skim off any foam that rises to the top. Add salt and pepper, cover, and simmer 3 to 4 hours.

Strain through a sieve into a bowl and refrigerate. Remove any congealed fat that rises to the surface.

Makes about 1 quart

Note : This stock will keep several days in a covered container in the refrigerator. To freeze, pour into a container and seal well; veal stock will keep for 2 months in the freezer.

Conversion Charts

WEIGHT MEASUREMENTS

Standard U.S.	Ounces	Metric
1 ounce	1	28 g
1/4 lb	4	113 g
1/2 lb	8	226 g
1 lb	16	454 g
1 1/2 lb	24	680 g
2 lb	37	908 g
2 1/2 lb	40	1134 g
3 lb	48	1367 g

VOLUME MEASUREMENTS

Standard U.S.		Ounces	Metric
1 tbs		1/2	15 ml
2 tbs		1	30 ml
3 tbs		1 1/2	45 ml
1/4 cup	4 tbs	2	60 ml
6 tbs		3	85 ml
1/2 cup	8 tbs	4	115 ml
1 cup		8	240 ml
1 pint	2 cups	16	480 ml
4 cups		32	960 ml

OVEN TEMPERATURES

Fahrenheit	Celsius
300°	148.8°
325°	162.8°
350°	177°
375°	190.5°
400°	204.4°
425°	218.3°
450°	232°

CONVERSION FACTORS

Ounces to grams:
Multiply the ounce figure by 28.3 to get the number of grams.

Pounds to grams:
Multiply the pound figure by 453.59 to get the number of grams.

Pounds to kilograms:
Multiply the pound figure by 0.45 to get the number of kilograms.

Ounces to milliliters:
Multiply the ounce figure by 30 to get the number of milliliters.

Cups to liters:
Multiply the cup figure by 0.24 to get the number of liters.

Fahrenheit to Celsius:
Subtract 32 from the Fahrenheit figure, multiply by 5, then divide by 9 to get the Celsius figure.

List of Contributors

Spain

EL CASTELL
Route de Lerida, Km. 129
E-25700 La Seu d'Urgell
Tel. 973-35.07.04
Fax 973-35.15.7

EL RACO DE CAN FABES
Sant Joan 6
E-08470 Sant Celoni
Tel. 93-867.28.51
Fax 93- 867.38.61

HACIENDA NA XAMENA
San Miguel
Apartado 423
E-07800 Ibiza
Tel. 971-33.30.46
Fax 971-33.31.75

HOSTAL DE LA GAVINA
E-17248 S'Agaró
Tel. 972-32.11.00
Fax 972- 32.15.73

HOTEL LA BOBADILLA
Finca La Bobadilla
E-18300 Loja-Granada
Tel. 958-32.18.61
Fax 958-32.18.10

HOTEL SANTA MARTA
Playa Santa Cristina
E-17310 Lloret de Mar
Tel. 972-36.49.04
Fax 972-36.92.80

LANDA PALACE
Carretera Madrid Irún, Km. 236
E-Burgos
Tel. 947-20.63.43
Fax 947-26.46.76

MARBELLA CLUB HOTEL
Carretera de Cadiz, Km. 178
E-29600 Marbella
Tel. 952-77.13.00
Fax 952-82.98.84

MAS DE TORRENT
E-17123 Torrent
Girona
Tel. 72-30.32.92
Fax 72-30.32.93

RESTAURANT JUAN ARZAK
Alto de Miracruz 21
E-20015 San Sebastián
Tel. 943-28.55.93
Fax 943-27.27.53

United States

BAY WOLF RESTAURANT
3853 Piedmont Avenue
Oakland, CA 94609
(510) 655-6004

CAFE BA-BA-REEBA!
2024 North Halsted Street
Chicago, IL 60614
(312) 935-5000

CAFE SEVILLE
2768 East Oakland Park Blvd.
Ft. Lauderdale, Florida 33306
(305) 565-1148

CAFE TU TU TANGO
CocoWalk
3015 Grand Avenue
Miami, Florida 33133
(305) 529-2222

COLUMBIA RESTAURANT
2117 East Seventh Avenue
Tampa, Florida 33605
(813) 248-3000

IBERIA RESTAURANT
190 Ladera Alpine Road
Portola Valley, CA 94028
(415) 854-1746

SOL Y LUNA
475 Sacramento Street
San Francisco, CA 94111
(415) 296-8696

Mail-Order Sources
for Special Ingredients
and Equipment

Corti Brothers
5810 Folsom Boulevard
Sacramento, CA 95819
(916) 736-3800

Catalán olive oil, Costa Brava anchovies,
saffron, and salt cod

Dean & DeLuca
560 Broadway
New York, NY 10012
(212) 431-1691, (in New York) ext. 223
(800) 221-7714, (outside New York state)

Spanish olive oil, saffron, and Valencian
short-grain rice

G.B. Ratto International Grocers
821 Washington Street
Oakland, CA 94607
(800) 228-3515 (in California)
(800) 325-3483 (outside California)

Spanish olive oil, saffron, salt cod fillets,
Valencian short-grain rice, and paella pans

La Española
2020 Lomita Boulevard, No. 6 and 7
Lomita, CA 90717
(310) 539-0455

Spanish cheeses, dry cured ham, olives,
olive oil, sausages, and paella pans

Williams-Sonoma
P.O. Box 7456
San Francisco, CA 94120
(800) 541-2233

Spanish clay casseroles, olive oil, saffron,
Valencian short-grain rice, and paella pans

Acknowledgments

This volume has been a wonderful learning experience for me. I would like to thank the many people in the United States and Spain who made it possible.

To guitarist Marc Teicholz, a perfectionist and a pleasure to work with. Bravo! To my musical engineer, Rainer Gembalczyk, for his patience and fortitude. Once again, thanks to Phil Edwards and George Horn. To composer Joaquin Nin-Culmell for information about his friends Ernesto Halffter and Manuel de Falla.

My deepest gratitude to all the chefs, proprietors, and managing directors of the restaurants, inns, and resorts who generously contributed menus and recipes to the cookbook. To Jose Luis and Jessica Relinque of Iberia Restaurant, new found friends who helped me through some of the more difficult recipes and explained Spanish

cooking terms. To Ginny Bouvier for help with the translations. To Jose Manuel Blanco of Sol y Luna Restaurant for showing me his kitchen and sharing his Manchego cheese.

I am so glad to have had Carolyn Miller as my editor once again; thank you for your attention to detail, expert advice, and culinary insights. To Suzie Skugstad for her wonderful design and her enthusiastic support of this project.

To Jim Armstrong; I couldn't ask for a better or more enthusiastic person to work with. To Ned Waring, for proofreading and keeping the volumes and Winston in motion; and to the rest of the gang at Menus and Music.

To my daughters Claire and Caitlin for their adventurous appetites and, to my husband John, thank you from the bottom of my heart.

Sharon O'Connor, creator of the *Menus and Music* series, is a musician, author, and cook. She was educated at the University of California, Berkeley and the Amsterdam Conservatory of Music. Ms. O'Connor is the cellist and founder of the San Francisco String Quartet. The *Menus and Music* series combines her love of music, food, and travel. *Music and Food of Spain* is her seventh book.

Marc Teicholz is one of the most promising classical guitarists of his generation. He was the first prizewinner of the 1989 International Guitar Foundation of America competition, has toured extensively in the United States and Canada, and has received critical acclaim for his recitals and master classes. He has a master's degree from the Yale School of Music and a J.D. from Boalt School of Law, University of California, Berkeley.